BUSEYISMS

Gary Busey

with Steffanie Sampson

BUSEYISMS

GARY BUSEY'S
BASIC
INSTRUCTIONS
BEFORE
LEAVING
EARTH

ST. MARTIN'S PRESS
NEW YORK

This book is dedicated to all of my relations.

www.stmartins.com

Designed by Jonathan Bennett

All photographs courtesy of the author,
unless otherwise noted.

Library of Congress Cataloging-in-Publication Data

Names: Busey, Gary, author. | Sampson, Steffanie, author.
Title: Buseyisms : Gary Busey's basic instructions before leaving earth / Gary
Busey with Steffanie Sampson.
Description: First edition. | New York : St. Martin's Press, [2018]

Identifiers: LCCN 2018013697 | ISBN 9781250161741 (hardcover) | ISBN
9781250213341 (signed edition) | ISBN 9781250161758 (ebook)
Subjects: LCSH: Busey, Gary--Anecdotes. | Actors--United States--Anecdotes.
Classification: LCC PN2287.B8845 A3 2018 | DDC 791.4302/8092--dc23
LC record available at https://lccn.loc.gov/2018013697

Our books may be purchased in bulk for promotional,
educational, or business use. Please contact your local bookseller or the
Macmillan Corporate and Premium Sales Department at
1-800-221-7945, extension 5442, or by email at
MacmillanSpecialMarkets@macmillan.com.

First Edition: September 2018

10 9 8 7 6 5 4 3 2 1

SEP 1 3 2018

This is the true story of my eccentric life so far, although some names and details have been changed.

Contents

Introduction

I've spent decades constructing "Buseyisms." What is a Buscyism? you ask. I create a deeper, more dimensional meaning for a word using the letters that spell it. For example, FART (a fan favorite): Feeling A Rectal Transmission. Another popular Buseyism is FUN: Finally Understanding Nothing. The Buseyism I cherish most is NUTS: Never Underestimate The Spirit. Many have said that my Buseyisms are insightful, motivational, and funny. The question often comes up: "Gary, when are you going to write a book with all your Buseyisms?"

Another commonly asked question is "Gary, when are you going to write a book about your life?"

Voilà! In this book, I do that and more. I tell the stories of my life, through my Buseyisms, *and* give the life lessons that I learned along the way. Wait a second, you're probably wondering, why? It is not to impress you or make you like me. I am sharing my stories to help inspire those of you who may be going through similar things to feel better. *Why would I take advice from Gary Busey?* you wonder. This is not advice. I am just a crazy, eccentric, loving person willing to share what I've learned after surviving the ups and downs of almost fifty years in Hollywood, a near-fatal motorcycle accident, a trip to the "afterlife," a drug overdose, two divorces, and a malignant tumor the size of a golf ball in the middle of my face. David Letterman once told me on his talk show that I am a living testimony to the resilience of the human body and spirit. So are you. I'm here to tell you, it is possible to go through terrible things and still come out a happy champion. This book is to help survivors everywhere to go on and live life fully. From my heart, my spirit, and my soul, I give to you my Buseyisms.

BUSEYISMS

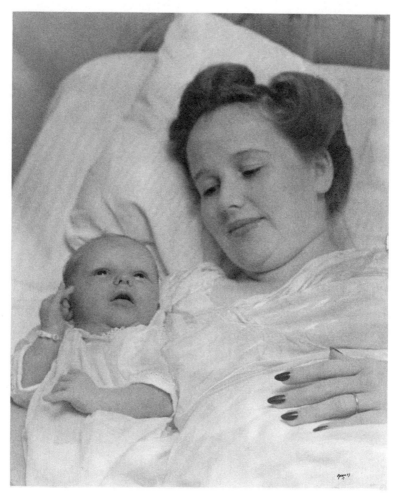

With Mom, Virginia "Ginny" Sadie Arnett Busey.

1. LOVE

Living On Victorious Energy

I ENTERED THE EARTH'S ATMOSPHERE at the Lillie-Duke
Hospital in Goose Creek, Texas, on June 29, 1944, at
11:50 A.M.—"just in time for lunch." My mom, Virginia
"Ginny" Sadie Arnett Busey, loved to tell me that. My dad,
Delmer Lloyd Busey, was not present for my arrival on earth
because he was in the South Pacific fighting in World War II.
Since Mom was on her own with a newborn baby, her sisters,
Ruth and Sis, helped raise me. Those three incredible
women were so nurturing, cuddly, and warm; they showered me with endless affection, doting on my every need. I
was the center of their universe. My feelings of that time
were infinitely rich with being loved every minute.

As a toddler, I loved to explore. Mom said I always went
where I wasn't supposed to go. She tried to contain me in a
playpen, but I always climbed out. Eventually, Mom turned
the playpen upside down to keep me secure, but I had
enough power in my one-year-old body to lift it up and escape. Then, I'd wander to the front door, where I found a
way of unlatching it. Once outside, I'd trek down the street

on my baby scooter to visit three dogs I was in love with. They always barked so loud when I arrived, I just knew they were telling me they loved me, too. Mom moved the latch higher on the front door, but I still found a way to un-lock it with a broomstick. Nothing could stop me from visiting those dogs. My mom and aunts all claimed, "We can't stop Gary. He goes where he wants to, and that's it." I was evolving into a real force of nature.

Aunts Ruth and Sis.

My favorite thing of all was when Mom showed me the picture of Dad that hung on the wall. She always lit up with an infec-tious smile that made me feel so happy while she en-thusiastically said, "That's your dad." Dad was the handsomest man I had ever seen—just like a movie star—a Victor Mature type. With one-quarter Native American blood, Dad had incredible smooth olive skin, thick black hair, and penetrating blue eyes. The thing that struck me the most about him was his tender smile. I couldn't wait to meet him in person. I knew he was going to be the most lov-ing dad ever.

My best friends at the end of the block, who would not
stop barking at me.

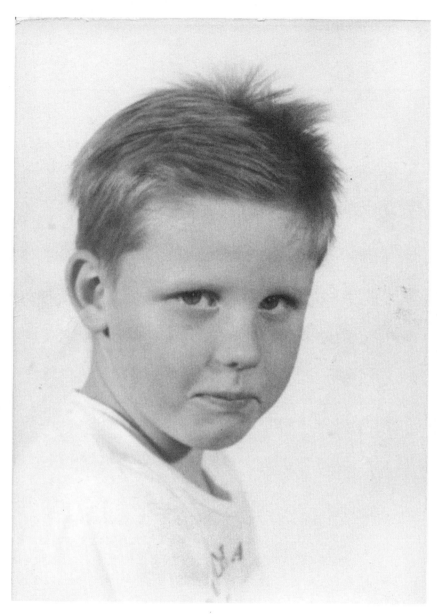

Me at the ripe old age of six.

2. FILM

Feelings Illuminated Like Magic

I N 1946, when I was almost two years old, Dad returned from World War II. He didn't waste any time getting reacquainted with Mom—within months of his return, she was pregnant with my sister, Carol, who was born on September 12, 1947.

Because of Dad's Seabee experience designing runways in the war, he got a design-construction job with the supermarket chain Safeway. After a few years on the job, Dad was promoted to management, which took the family from Goose Creek, Texas, to Chickasha, Oklahoma, in 1950. I attended kindergarten in Chickasha, but just a year later, Dad moved the family again, this time to Oklahoma City.

In Oklahoma City, just four blocks from our new home, on the corner of Western and Tenth Street, was a movie theater called the Wes-Ten. The Wes-Ten was the local baby-sitter to kids of all ages in the neighborhood. Every weekend from noon to six, the 350-seat theater was packed to the brim with excitable, rowdy kids of all ages. Mom gave me thirty cents, then sent me off with my buddies Ronnie Dale,

Bobby Hughes, John Mason, and Tommy Hawke to spend the day at the Wes-Ten. The five of us raced the four blocks, through a park, around trees, and over fences, to be the first one to arrive. I was six years old and feeling free as a bird.

The Wes-Ten became my private paradise. On the outside, the façade was outlined in neon with a V-shaped flashing marquee. Inside, down the sides of the theater walls and all through the lobby were large framed pictures of the biggest Hollywood movie stars of the day, like John Wayne, Jennifer Jones, Jerry Lewis, Dean Martin, Jean Arthur, Joel McCrea, Jane Russell, and Marilyn Monroe. Looking at the pictures, I felt like I knew each and every one of them personally. Then there was the lobby concession stand. It was the most glorious sight—like being in Candy Land with every delicious treat of the day imaginable—Baby Ruths, PayDays, Milky Ways, Snickers, Junior Mints, Milk Duds, Raisinets—and of course popcorn with butter. I always got a Coca-Cola and popcorn with Milk Duds; I loved mixing them together.

In 1951, it cost a dime to get into the theater, a dime for popcorn, a nickel for candy, and a nickel for soda pop. I carried my treasured lunch, stepping on the sticky candy-covered floor, to the most perfect seat I could find. I felt the excitement building inside as the lights went down. The lavish red-and-gold curtains opened to reveal the big silver movie screen. Then—*bam!*—there was the logo of the movie studio in conjunction with its iconic theme song blasting through the building. I was so moved when I heard that music booming, my heart swelled, bringing tears to my eyes. Sitting there in the dark, I felt like I was in heaven on earth.

With Mom and Dad.

I was so taken aback by the people lit up on the screen. They became real to me as I watched them talk, dance, fight, shoot, and love. In my six-year-old mind, I was in the movie, and the people on the screen were my best friends. Emotions stirred in me that I never felt before. Without knowing it consciously, watching the movies was giving me a vision of life in a crash course. There were no ratings, no parental discretions advised. I was six, watching shoot-'em-up westerns, crime dramas, and thrillers. When I saw *The Thing* with my best friend, Ronnie Dale, I remember we were so scared, we moved all the way back to share the very last seat in the theater in case we had to make a run for it.

It was an all-day event beginning with serials like *The Perils of Pauline*, followed by twelve Looney Tunes cartoons, then the double feature. When we left the movies, the five of us walked home, through the park, hopping fences, shooting behind trees, acting out the movies we just saw,

My best friend in all of life,
my sister, Carol.

each choosing his favorite character to play. I was always the hero.

When I was seven years old, knowing how much I loved the movies, Mom said, "Gary, there's a very special movie that I want you to see called *Samson and Delilah*." Since it wasn't playing at the Wes-Ten, Mom took me to a different theater across town, which was a big deal. I was transfixed, just as Mom thought I would be. Watching *Samson and Delilah* moved me so deeply, it was like lightning struck my artistic heart in a way that gave me the freedom and desire to express myself.

When the movie was over, I asked Mom, "Where do all the people go?"

"This audience goes out, and a new audience comes in."

"No, not those people. The people up there on the screen."

"They go off and make another picture show for us to see."

"Hmm." I thought about that concept for a moment, then announced, "That's what I want to do."

"Oh, you want to be in the picture show?"

"I want to tell stories with light."

3. STRONG

Stretching To Reach
Opportunities Not Given

GROWING UP, home life was very simple—Mom always in the kitchen baking, family meals at the table, church every Sunday. We were your typical American family in the '50s. Mom and Dad were very much in love and extremely close. When Dad wasn't working, they were together, golfing, square-dancing, or playing bridge. Dad gave Mom the freedom of going out in the evenings to sewing clubs with the ladies, and in return, Mom gave Dad the freedom to play golf whenever he wanted. As construction-design manager for Safeway stores in three states, Dad frequently traveled for business. On the road, he always wrote Mom love letters telling her he couldn't wait to get back home to her. They were like teenagers in love. By the time I was eight years old, I had a little brother named David.

Mom, a Debbie Reynolds type, had fair skin, strawberry-blond hair, hazel-green eyes, and a petite build. Half-Irish, half-English, she was feisty and energetic. With her three Busey children, she dealt with the whole gamut of personalities. David, a natural redhead, small for his age but sturdy, was friendly and happy, always thoughtful before he acted. Carol, cute and quirky with brownish auburn hair and glasses since second grade, was slow and careful, reserved and shy, not one to put herself out there. I, on the other hand, was always loud, fast, and carefree, never thinking before I spoke and *always* doing something to be noticed. Growing up, my interests were very simple; in fact, I really had only one—*football.*

The first time I remember playing football, I was on a team in the third grade while attending Buchanan Elementary in Oklahoma City. It quickly became my passion. But in 1953, Dad moved the family again for work, this time to Tulsa, Oklahoma, where football wasn't available until eighth grade.

When I finally made it to eighth grade, the only thing on my mind was getting on our school football team, the Bell Bobcats. Their coach, Chuck Boyd, happened to live across the street from us, so I was a definite shoo-in for the team. I went to tryouts confident that I would be victorious, but to my surprise, I didn't make the team. That is when football changed from a passion to an obsession. All I had on my mind was making that football team. I wanted Dad to be proud of me. You see, Dad was an all-American high school football player. He even earned a football scholarship at the University of Arkansas. I wouldn't rest until I was playing football on a team—like Dad.

My challenge was my size. I was considerably smaller than every other player. However, that didn't deter me. I spent every waking moment practicing football. I practiced with anyone I could find, even my little brother and sister. David, who was eight years my junior, toughed it out in the yard, sporting a little football outfit with a tiny helmet, following my lead, running up and down as we dodged each other. I also practiced my tackles on my unwilling sister, Carol, who was three years my junior. Whenever she heard the word "Hut!" coming from me, no matter where she was in the house, she knew she had to run for safety—usually locking herself in the bathroom—because I was charging through the house to tackle her.

In the ninth grade, I tried out for the team again with

Richard David Busey.

high hopes and a strong will. I made it! I was given the position of starting center. During the year I was on the team, I learned great new techniques that made me a better player. I even created a special way of snapping the ball, which flipped it in a spiral, landing the ball right into the punter's hands. It became my signature snap. I loved football so much, if I could have turned myself into a football, I would have.

In the tenth grade, when I started a new school, Nathan Hale High, I got demoted to the *junior* varsity team with the rest of the smaller guys. Being on the junior team was devoid of any reward. I felt inferior. *I had to get on the main team.* I was relentless in preparing myself for next year's tryouts, practicing the drills over and over. I worked on improving my speed, my agility, even my tolerance to pain. I became a football machine.

STRONG

The starting center at Nathan Hale High
School, Tulsa, Oklahoma, 1962.

Next season when tryouts came, my athletic ability was
at its peak, but I was still smaller than everyone. I hadn't
grown an inch. At tryouts, the coach, Larry Miller, handed
the players salt tabs. Not knowing that I was supposed to
swallow it with water, I sucked on it. Right away, I fell to my
knees, spewing vomit all over the field. Coach approached
me with a concerned look, then said, "Are you sure you
want to play football?"

"Yes. I *have* to play football."

Coach didn't ask why; he just stood there sizing me up. I
stared right back at him with vomit dripping off my chin.
As we both gazed at each other without blinking, I noticed

BUSEYISMS

he had a very kind face. The face of a hero. His posture, energy, and exuberance were strong. He was the type of coach you really wanted to please. Finally, after a minute passed, Coach gave me a smile, flashing bigger pearly whites than mine—if you can imagine that. "Okay, get up!" he ordered. During tryouts, Coach pushed me hard. He knew exactly what to do to bring out the best in me. In the end, Coach gave me a position on the first team, starting center, number 55. Over the next two years, Coach guided me in a loving and powerful way to be a champion.

As of this writing, I am still in touch with Coach Miller. The last time I saw him was in March of 2018. He was his usual strong, exuberant self.

With Coach Larry Miller in Tulsa, Oklahoma, 2016.
(Courtesy of Steffanie Sampson)

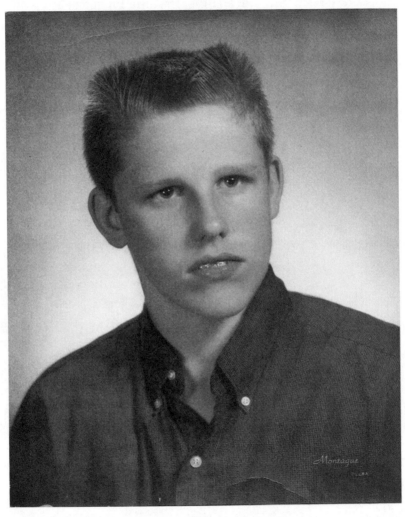

My eighth-grade Bell Junior High School picture,
Tulsa, Oklahoma, 1958.

4. DARE

Doing A Radical Experiment

THE FOOTBALL TEAM DEVELOPED A GREAT CAMA-
RADERIE. Together we were a solid unit, a real brotherhood. I was the team clown, always cracking jokes, doing
anything to make the guys laugh. Everything was funny to
me. One day, as we were getting ready for practice, the team
surrounded me in the locker room, holding up a flyer for the
upcoming school play. They said, "Gary, we want you to go
out for this play." I had seen casting notices all around campus, on every wall, in every corner: "*South Pacific* . . .
South Pacific . . . *South Pacific*." However, my main purpose was football, nothing else. Acting was the last thing
on my mind. When I wasn't thinking about football, I was
thinking about girls. Connie, Janet, and Patsy, to be specific.
This really threw me for a loop.

"What?" I asked.

"You're a funny guy. We want you to audition for *South
Pacific*."

"No!"

But the team kept on pushing, trying different tactics, taunting me, telling me I was too scared . . . I didn't have the guts. They finally got my attention when they said, "We *dare* you!"

"You *dare* me?" One thing you should know about me: If you ever dare me to do anything, I'm doing it. It's fun to be part of a good dare because when you have a strong heart, a strong mind, and a strong will, you're gonna take it on. "Okay, I will." I snatched the flyer.

When I went to the tryout for the play, I was in uncharted waters. It was very unusual for football players to mix with drama students. I was clueless about what to do. Inside the theater was bustling with activity, kids tinkering with lights and trying on costumes. There were probably thirty people sitting in the audience with pads of paper and scripts. The director handed me a scene. "Here, try the part of Private Victor Jerome." She paired me up with a guy I knew named Harlan. "You guys will be next, oh, and do this song, too." She handed me another paper. I had no problem with singing; I'd sung in church every Sunday since I was a little boy. Singing was my favorite part of the service, which was definitely going to be a plus here.

This dare was getting exciting.

Harlan and I had a minute to look at the scene, then the director said, "Okay, go!" When I stepped on the stage, I felt oddly at home. After I said my first line, everyone in the audience chuckled. I didn't know if that was good or bad; I wasn't sure if the line was supposed to be funny. I knew nothing about acting, except you get up and talk loud. I said the next line, and some audience members changed their seats to be closer to the stage. When we finished the scene, everybody was laughing and clapping at us. I didn't think

I'd done anything special. All I did was say the words. I left the audition satisfied; I'd completed the dare and had fun along the way. I certainly didn't expect or want to get the part.

Two days later, for the heck of it, I checked the bulletin board to see who got cast. My jaw dropped. There it was as clear as day: *Private Victor Jerome—Gary Busey*! I couldn't believe my eyes. A feeling of excitement came over me (in a tough football player–type of way). It was a surprisingly beautiful moment of accomplishment that I initially didn't think was important, but I found out in that moment, it really was. Because of a stupid dare, I achieved something I never would have imagined possible. I was now playing the part of Private Victor Jerome and looking forward to it.

This dare was just beginning.

In the springtime—with football season over—I switched gears from football to theater. I was astonished at how comfortable I felt with the theater folk. They were a creative and kind group. The way the rehearsal process worked was fascinating—one scene or one musical number at a time, then blocking, props, costumes, finally putting everything together. Acting was the antithesis of football. I was gardening in a new oasis of expressive freedom that I had never been in before. I loved it.

When opening night came, I was chomping at the bit to get onstage, like a stallion at the starting gate ready to charge. Here we were in the dark of night, taking on the life of another person, wearing different clothes, entering a different world that we were about to share with our families, the faculty, the students—*and the football team.* The school band played music as I watched people pile into the auditorium, until there was nowhere left to sit. Seeing that full house and hearing the murmurs of the crowd sent a gust of energy surging through my body, like electricity in a rainstorm.

Once the play started, I entered *the zone,* where your mind and body merge together and everything happens automatically without thought. It was a euphoric place to be. Private Victor Jerome had arrived, and Gary Busey left the building. I did my part seamlessly, and every time I spoke, the audience laughed. Hearing people laugh *at me* was sheer joy. The acceptance I received onstage went forever to my heart. That night, the theater made its way into my blood. This was more than simply a dare; it was angelic intervention.

After *South Pacific,* I became known all over high school as "the funny Victor Jerome who made people laugh." When people saw me at school, they pointed, laughing, and said, "Hey, there he is." It was my first taste of being recognized not just for being me but for something I did onstage that people loved and applauded.

5. PAST

Preoccupation About Spent Time

IN THE FALL OF 1963, I earned a football scholarship to go to college at Coffeyville Junior College in Kansas. For the first time, I was living on my own away from home. After a few weeks, I went back to visit the family (with a considerable amount of dirty laundry). I grabbed my bag of dirty clothes from the car, but Dad stopped me in the driveway. "Put those dirty clothes back in your car. They have washers and dryers where you live. You're out of the nest now. You have to learn how to fly on your own."

"Yes, sir."

I realized things were changing. The days of living at home, with Mom doing my laundry, were in the past. I never went back again with dirty laundry.

At Coffeyville, my main focus was football and a girl named Judy. I met Judy at our first football game. At first glance, I was spellbound. Here was this intriguing blond girl wearing short red shorts, a tiny-fringed red shirt, sporting a large bird helmet (resembling our Red Raven mascot) that covered her face. I couldn't take my eyes off her; I had to see her face. When she finally removed the large bird helmet, my heart leaped out of my chest. Standing before me was the most beautiful girl on the face of the planet. "She's mine," I vowed. We started dating right away. After a year, we were a full-fledged couple.

Coffeyville Junior College starting team.

Judy was a year ahead of me in school. When she finished Coffeyville, she transferred to Kansas State College of Pittsburg, leaving me behind. As soon as I could, I transferred to Kansas State, too, with another football scholarship. Things were going great at Kansas State, until one day at practice, while I was catching a pass, the cleats in my left shoe got caught in the ground. The force sent me smashing down, and I busted the medial meniscus in my right knee and tore the ligaments and tendons in my ankle. This caused me to lose my athletic scholarship and forced me to put football in the past, for good.

At first, I struggled with the notion that I couldn't play football anymore, but soon I realized I couldn't let the past consume me, because it was gone, never to come back. Crying about what happened wouldn't help me or change what happened. I had to move on. I turned to the only other thing I knew I could do—theater. I auditioned for a dramatic scholarship at Oklahoma State University—and got in.

Playing at the Red Dog Saloon in Reseda, California, 1966.

6. BAND

Bringing A New Direction

NOW THAT I HAD MOVED TO OKLAHOMA STATE, I needed a place to stay. While at Kansas State, I had joined the Sigma Chi fraternity, so I went to the Sigma Chi house at Oklahoma State to see if I could get a room. The president of the fraternity, Glen Mitchell (who had mustard all over his face from eating a hot dog), met me outside. He noticed that I had a drum set in my car. Surprised, he asked, "Are you a drummer?"

"Yes," I replied. I wasn't really a drummer, but I wanted to be. I had tried out for a few bands but got rejected every time.

"We have a band here, but we need a drummer." Glen, who played piano, brought me into the house and introduced me to the rest of the band: Charlie Swain on guitar, and John Crowder on bass guitar. John also made the best lizard face I'd ever seen—a talent every band needs.

I joined them immediately.

It was a perfect fit. I knew different musical arrangements from the Beatles, the Beach Boys, the Turtles, and the

Association, among others. Since I was the only one who knew the words, I became the singer, too. For the next year, we played around campus and got really good. We even learned to sing a cappella. We became the top band around, doing hit songs like "Along Comes Mary," "Never My Love," "Cherish," "Happy Together," and "My Girl." We were so hugely popular on campus that we had to give our band a name. A friend in the Sigma Chi house suggested, "How about the Rubber Band?" That sounded good to us, so we became *the Rubber Band*.

In 1966, I had the idea to take the Rubber Band to California for the summer. I knew we could have a music career. The guys agreed. We hitched a yellow trailer to Glen's pea-green 1959 Chevrolet station wagon, loaded our equipment, and said good-bye to our friends and family. Dad was outside planting a tree.

"We're leaving for California."

Being Native American, Dad never spoke much, but when he did, his words were very poignant. So far in my life, he had taught me two simple lessons: "Boys don't cry," and "*Can't* never did do nothing." I lived by those lessons, and they had been very helpful to me growing up. I waited for Dad to reply, but he didn't stop what he was doing or look up at me. He forcefully thrust his shovel in the ground and finally said, "You can do anything you want to do." Then he took a long pause and said, "And if you want it done right, do it yourself." He carefully placed the new tree in the hole he'd dug and covered the roots with dirt. Dad never looked at me.

I left my childhood home with Dad's words close to my heart. They became the basic bricks of my foundation.

With fifty dollars in my pocket, I drove with the Rubber Band to California on the original Route 66, stopping three times to eat and get gas. We made it there in less than two days. I had thirteen dollars and sixty-seven cents left.

California was completely different from Oklahoma. I'd heard of the hippies, but seeing them firsthand was awesome, like being at a carnival on acid. They wore bell-bottom pants, wide belts, paisley shirts with psychedelic colors, necklaces with peace signs, and round rose-colored glasses. The polar opposite of us fresh-faced cowboys from Oklahoma, the hippies were cartoonlike tree people that lived outside under the oaks, dancing around burning incense, smoking things that made them sing songs about peace and flowers. We stood out like farm animals.

Determined to get the Rubber Band a record deal, I had a list of ten managers in my pocket. One by one, we got rejected by all of them—except for the last guy, Buddy Resnik. Buddy had a personal management company in Beverly Hills called National Talent Consultants. He was big-time; he represented actress Nichelle Nichols on a new show called *Star Trek* and an Irish band called Them with Van Morrison, who had the hit "Gloria" on the radio. We decided to show up at his office even though we couldn't get an appointment. Buddy, a buoyant young man a little older than I was, bald, with a big build, and wire-rimmed glasses, took one look at us and asked, "Where are you guys from?" I guess he could tell we weren't from Southern California.

I was the spokesperson. I told Buddy, "We have a great following in Oklahoma. We're really good. We want to get a record deal."

"Do you have a tape?"

We had nothing. "Let us sing a cappella for you."

"Sure, go ahead."

The four of us sang a couple of Beach Boys songs a cappella. We sounded great, but Buddy didn't sign us—however, he took a liking to us. He invited us to join him at the Whisky a Go Go on Sunset Boulevard to see Them play.

The Whisky a Go Go was packed wall to wall with stoned hippies. There were movies of live hydras and amoebas moving around inside giant protoplasms splattered on the walls. I felt like I was inside the belly of an unknown animal on an unknown planet. There were scantily clad go-go dancers in cages high up on poles, wearing boots to the top of their calves, with little panties, bikini tops, and feather boas, bouncing and grooving. The guys had long hair with headbands, long beards, tattoos, and no shirts. As crazy as everyone looked, once again, we were the ones who stood out sporting our Rubber Band performing uniform: blue blazers, white jeans, and white saddle oxford shoes.

We sat with Buddy and Paul Rothchild, manager of the opening act—a new band called the Doors. When the Doors played, I thought they were awful. I leaned over to Glen and whispered, "I think we may be on the wrong trail ride here." Then Them came on. They were incredible. I took this unbelievable opportunity to ask Buddy as many questions as possible about the music industry. Buddy answered each question fully with sincerity. Before the night was over, Buddy said, "Give me a phone number, I'll see what I can do."

A few days later, Buddy called with a gig at a club geared toward the younger crowd in the valley. "You're not going to

The Rubber Band in our performing uniform.

get paid. You may get drinks and a hamburger, but at least you can go out and show your stuff." We sucked—big-time.

After we played, I got so upset with myself, I ran to the car to cry where no one could see me. I called Buddy later that evening, still crying. "They didn't like our music."

Buddy had no sympathy. "Well, good, you got a taste of Southern California music. It's no big deal. We'll find something else for you."

As promised, Buddy got us another gig, at the Red Dog Saloon in Reseda near San Fernando Valley State College.

Buddy laid it down. "They charge at the door, and whatever they make, you get to keep—but you've got to be good. It's a real rowdy crowd." We were good. The college students liked our music. We made sixty dollars to share between the four of us. It was thrilling to be making money in the music business in California, even if it was only fifteen dollars each. We played in that club every night that summer until it was time to go back home. Driving back to Oklahoma on Route 66, I carried unlimited possibilities in my heart. Dad was right: I could do anything I wanted—even make money in the music industry.

For the next year, back in Oklahoma, all I heard on the radio was "Light My Fire" by the Doors. They were pretty out there on psychedelic flavors, but the song grew on me. It reminded me that I really belonged in California. I told Glen, "We weren't on the wrong trail ride after all. I just didn't recognize the cows."

7. WIFE

Wanted In Forever Eternity

IN THE SUMMER OF 1967, I dropped out of college, just one class short of graduation, to move to California with the Rubber Band. Charlie Swain opted not to go so we replaced him with a new guitar player, Ronnie Getman. The first thing I did was call Buddy Resnik. Buddy signed the Rubber Band to our very first management contract. He got our name out there, but no record labels had any interest in us, so essentially, we continued where we left off the summer before—playing dive bars anywhere we could. As the relentless leader of the band, I didn't wait for Buddy to get us gigs; I went out myself and got some, too. Eventually, we landed jobs at really cool places like Disneyland's Tomorrowland Stage and Knott's Berry Farm. But we were too rowdy for Disneyland and got fired. We also got fired from Knott's Berry Farm because we were blamed for starting a fight between a group of hippies and a group of Marines. That didn't stop us. We kept on keeping on.

In 1968, we decided to change our name. The Rubber Band gave an image of bobby-soxers, bubble gum, and bouffant hairdos, which absolutely didn't work in California. I came up with the name Bordyne after my dorm in college. Pretty soon, we saved enough money to rent a beautiful flat-roof, four-bedroom house on Tendilla Avenue in Woodland Hills.

One day, while we were practicing in the garage, the phone rang. It was my girlfriend, Judy, back in Kansas. We spoke our usual pleasantries, then out of the blue, Judy said, "It's time for us to get married."

"What?"

"I want to be your wife!"

Where was this coming from? I had grown to love Judy very much in our six years together. However, we had been growing apart during the year I lived in California. We became extremely long-distance (sometimes speaking to each other only once a month). Playing music was my priority. All my hard efforts leading the band were just starting to pay off. We had been gaining a lot of momentum. I didn't even have time for a girlfriend, let alone a wife. The band had become my family. Don't get me wrong; Judy was always in the back of my mind, but I had big musical dreams to fulfill. "What do you mean?" I asked.

I knew what she meant; I was just stalling for time trying to wrap my head around it.

"I'll tell you what I mean. We've been dating almost six years now, and you need to shit or get off the pot. When you come back to Tulsa for the Christmas holidays, we're going to get married."

"I'll be on tour with the band."

"I don't care. You can take one day off. Marry me now or I'm going to start dating."

I'd never heard her speak so forcefully, which is probably

The Rubber Band signing our first management contract with Buddy Resnick.

why I caved in right away. "Okay, okay, yeah, we'll marry on the one day the band has off." As I uttered those words, panic flooded my body. I did not feel ready to get married . . . to anyone.

Nonetheless, on December 30, 1968—between gigs in Tulsa—the band and I drove sixty miles to Coffeyville, Kansas, so Judy and I could get married. I endured a ninety-minute ceremony at an Episcopal church in front of family, friends, and the band. It felt like I was put in a slingshot and hurled out to the sky only to plummet back to earth as a

Our self-made publicity.

husband. There was no festive party or reception following our long day in church. We went to Judy's house with her family and my parents to get her stuff. I opened the garage to load her many bags in the car, and my stomach sank. The words *Just Married, Forever as One* were spray-painted on the back. It knocked the wind out of me. *Deep breaths, Gary.* Everything I did took deep breaths. I kept thinking, *What next? What next?* I took tiny little steps, each one hard to make, but finally got the car packed up.

Forever?

I got in *our* Chevy and took my "plus one" to the Camelot Inn, also known as the Cram-a-Lot In. The Cram-a-Lot, built to look like King Arthur's castle, was a popular hotel in Tulsa with the young people who went there after proms and dances to get a room. Our luxurious honeymoon suite had big plush chairs you could sink into, billowing yellow curtains, a king-sized bed, and a view overlooking Interstate 44, where the road leaves Tulsa toward Oklahoma City. I stared out the window. Everything looked different—the Tulsa skyline, the streets, the trees. Even I looked different in my reflection. No longer a carefree warrior of life, I had a wife. The responsibilities I had just taken on, to this loving partner who entrusted her "forever" with me—and now carried my last name—weighed heavily on my mind.

With Judy Busey at Disneyland.

8. GUIDE

Giving Understanding
In Detailed Experience

E VERYBODY ON THIS PLANET IS AN ACTOR, one way or another—it comes with being human. I didn't come to California to be an actor, but after working so hard with the band for so little reward, I thought acting might be another river to sail on. I always had a deep fascination with movies since childhood, so I started reading articles in the paper about auditions. I didn't go to any of the auditions until I found a notice that really stood out to me: "James Best looking for new talent at Screen Gems." Screen Gems was bigtime. They produced the shows I grew up watching, like *Father Knows Best, The Donna Reed Show, Gidget,* and *Dennis the Menace.* I had a good feeling about this notice. It practically jumped off the page, so I made an appointment.

When I met James Best, coordinator of new talent at Screen Gems, I recognized him from various war movies and Westerns I'd seen growing up. The way he said lines, with a country twang like I had, made me feel right at home. In person, he was remarkably handsome, strong, and charismatic. I was incredibly impressed to be in the company of an accomplished character actor with such star power.

I told Jimmy of my history in classical theater at Oklahoma State University, that I was a drummer in a working band, and of my desire to see where I could go in acting. Then I offered to do three scenes and a monologue I had prepared for him.

"No, not now. Have you ever been in a workshop?" he asked.

"Well, I've had metal class and woodshop."

"No, no, I mean for acting."

"Can you teach acting?"

"It's film awareness and camera technique, how you work on a set for a motion picture or television show."

"I was trained in classical theater."

"That's the opposite." He gave me a brief synopsis of his workshop. As I listened to him speak so genuinely, unlike most of the people I'd met in California, my heart started dancing. I knew I was in the right company. I joined his workshop.

The workshop met every Wednesday and Friday night from 7:00 to 10:00 P.M. on Chandler Boulevard in North Hollywood. The small room was buzzing with animated actors chatting as they took their seats. Then Jimmy introduced me to the group. "We have a new student—Gary Busey." He focused all his attention on me and asked, "Are you ready to do that monologue you mentioned in the office?"

"Yes."

"What's it from?"

"*The Rainmaker*. Burt Lancaster."

"Let's hear it."

I walked onto the stage—it was small with one table, a bench, a few chairs, and a faux front entrance door. I sat on the bench, took ten seconds to focus, then began projecting my voice to the back row of the parking lot. I didn't get through my first sentence before Jimmy interrupted me, nodding. "You *have* done a lot of theater."

"Yeah. That's called projecting, so they'll hear me in the back row."

"I'm aware of that. You see, in movies we have little microphones so you can just do it softly. Keep it simple, be yourself, and talk naturally." Within five minutes of his workshop, I learned my most valuable lesson: Keep it simple and be yourself.

I became very engrossed in Jimmy's workshop. His lessons were all designed to help the actor steal the show. I learned at lightning speed, absorbing every minute detail of his class, but I got my most valuable lessons after hours. Most nights, Jimmy stayed with me after class until 11:30 or 12:00. He taught me where to stand, correct posture, head positioning, sitting, eye movements, all to optimize camera time in all types of shots. I hung on his every word. I especially loved to hear about his past movie experiences.

He quickly became my mentor.

Jimmy saw promise in me. He knew I had something before I knew I had anything. I could feel love coming with his direction—but he was tough, too. One night, we were working past the clock and he was trying to explain a camera technique on how to put the body in a place where you could cast shadows on the other actors so they would lose their shot and you could steal the scene. I kept asking him questions, then interrupting with more questions because I just couldn't grasp the concept. Finally, Jimmy said, "Do you want to get three-buttoned?"

"No." I had no idea what he meant by "three-buttoned," but the way he said it, it didn't sound good.

"Then you'd better listen to me."

"I am listening."

"No, you're talking a lot."

"Well, I have a lot of questions."

"Don't ask them until I'm finished talking."

"Okay. What's 'three-button'?"

He pointed to the third button on my shirt, then—*boom*—whipped a swift jab faster than the strike of a rattlesnake, landing his fist on the third button just at my sternum. "If you don't listen, I'll three-button ya right here, and you won't be able to breathe for five minutes."

"I don't want to be three-buttoned."

"Okay, then let's continue." He wanted to let me know he was in charge. He was. I was his lieutenant, and he was my major general in the army of show biz.

We went on for a bit, and then I asked him a question I'd been asking since I started his workshop. "Jimmy, when can I get an agent?"

His reply was always the same: "When I tell you you're ready."

About a year and a half into the workshop, my classmate asked if I would find a scene to do with her for the Actors Studio. I selected a scene from the one-act play *Hello Out There!* by William Saroyan about a down-on-his-luck gambler and an unhappy cook who fall in love. During our performance, my classmate forgot her lines, so I took over to keep the scene going and improvised a different ending. When we finished, a deep voice with a low timbre boomed from the dark audience, "Gary Busey, where are you from?" Although I couldn't see him, I recognized his voice instantly from one of my favorite movies, *The Carpetbaggers*. It was George Peppard.

"Texas and Oklahoma."

"How long have you studied acting?"

"A year and a half."

"Have you been in movies yet?"

"No."

"Do you want to?"

"Yeah."

"Well, that was very good." His compliment went straight to my heart. It still lives there. The next day, with my head a little inflated from George Peppard's flattery, I asked Jimmy, "Can I go see an agent yet?"

His reply was still the same: "When I tell you you're ready."

It had been three years since I began Jimmy's workshop, and still Jimmy would not let me see an agent. My class-mate Helby had finally gotten her permission to see an agent, and she asked me to be her scene partner. Since it was up to Jimmy to decide, I asked him, "Can I please do it?"

Jimmy gave me a long, piercing gaze, then said, "You're ready to see an agent now." His words sent chills all over my body inside and out. Getting Jimmy's permission was a huge feather in my cap of achievement.

The agent was Glen Shaw, a large, affable older man running his own smaller talent agency. Even though it was not meant to be my meeting and I was neon green in the industry, the agent wanted me—not Helby. Jimmy told Glen, "In order for Gary to be your client, you need to have him on the street tomorrow with interviews."

The next day, Glen got me my first job interview, for a part as a day player on a Western television show called *The High Chaparral,* starring Leif Erickson and Cameron Mitchell. It was the part of a guy who hits Leif in the face with a stick while he's sleeping. There were no lines.

When I got to the casting office, it was a cattle call packed with young hopefuls like me. In the waiting room, I watched actor after actor come and go, spending about three minutes apiece, each doing the audition around five times. I could hear the casting director give the same instruction again and again through the partition: "Look at the clock on the wall. After casting says the line, 'Where did he go?' look on the opposite side of the wall at a picture so we can see how your expression changes." When it was my turn, I got the same instruction. Unlike all the actors before me, she only had me do it once. I didn't change my expression. The casting director said, "Okay, great. You can go now." I got the job—because my expression didn't change. All the other actors did too much. I kept it simple the way Jimmy taught me.

For my first job, Jimmy gave me very specific on-set instructions. "I want you to go to the head of every department, introduce yourself, tell them this is your first job, and ask if there is anything you can do to help them. That'll make you part of the crew before you start shooting." On set, I did as Major General Jimmy ordered. It worked out great. It made the crew want to help me. The camera heads put me in positions where I'd be in every shot. Then they started throwing lines at me. "Gary, you say this since you're standing behind Cameron." I ended up with three days of work and seven lines because of Jimmy's guidance. James Best single-handedly helped me secure my first job and a place in this industry of motion pictures.

Writing music with Jake Busey.

9. CHANGE

Creating Happiness And
New Guiding Energy

EVEN THOUGH I WAS NOW PURSUING AN ACTING CAREER, I also still relentlessly chased a career in music. Our band, now called Bordyne, continued to book gigs anywhere we could. One particular night, at a dive bar in the valley called the Image on Reseda Boulevard next to the 101 Freeway, motorcyclists were actually riding their bikes inside the club on the dance floor, revving their engines, spinning their back tires, doing burnouts while the band played. The bikers turned their headlights on our faces, screaming, "Play 'Louie Louie'!" They forced us to play "Louie Louie" over and over for two hours straight. Finally, I told my bandmate Ronnie, "You know what? I feel like trash fish caught in a net here. We should call ourselves Carp." And so the band changed its name to Carp.

The next few years brought a lot more change. Buddy Resnik left the management business, which left Carp unrepresented. Eventually, though, I found a producer, Daniel Moore, interested in cutting an album with us. We recorded it in an old studio off Vine Street in Hollywood, next to the Capitol Records building, called Gold Star. Our record turned out surprisingly better than I'd anticipated. When it was finished, Daniel passed it along to various record companies, hoping to strike a deal. Shortly after, we got a call from him. "Epic Records wants to release your album."

"Really? What do we have to do?"

"Nothing. They're going to release it as is."

And just like that, our position in the music industry changed—we were "recording artists with Epic Records."

Carp's record was released on the spot. I felt an incredible feeling when I heard our song on the radio for the first time. All our hard work had finally paid off. Up until now, Judy had been supporting us working as an executive secretary. I hoped this record deal would bring in enough money so I could start supporting her. Unfortunately, that didn't happen. Our record didn't get enough publicity. Eventually, it fizzled out and we got shelved. Just like that, our position in the music industry changed again—we were back in the garage.

In September 1970, while the band was rehearsing in the garage, Judy dropped by to give me some news. With a very straight, serious face, she said, "The rabbit is dead" (a euphemism for a positive old-fashioned pregnancy test). Nine months later, on June 15, 1971, William Jacob Busey entered the earth's atmosphere. This change was great. Jake brought a sense of joy to me that I'd never felt before. He was the sweetest little person I had ever encountered, with a perpetual smile and an exceptionally playful nature. He loved to be tickled, but most of all, he adored it when I did silly faces and made funny noises, which I did a lot. I'd look

Recording with the band.

at him for hours and hours, astonished at the human being that I helped to create.

Being a father was a miracle and a blessing that automatically put fire in my engine to do better. I already had fire inside of me naturally, but now it was an inferno. Right off the bat, I started booking more acting jobs, one right after the other. It dawned on me, after I finished a movie called *Hex* in South Dakota with Keith Carradine and Scott Glenn, that acting was happening for me a lot easier than music. I met the guys from Carp and told them I was leaving the band. It was shocking for them, but it was a change we were all ready for—the end of Carp.

At the time, I was happy with my agent, Glen Shaw. He had been doing very well for me, but Jimmy Best knew I could do better. He got me an invitation to meet Meyer

Mishkin, agent to such notable character actors as Richard Dreyfuss, Charles Bronson, James Coburn, Lee Marvin, and Jim Davis. Meyer, a likeable, tiny, silver-haired Jewish man with a very round face who was in his early sixties, welcomed me to his office. He made me feel so comfortable, I reclined in his chair, put my feet up, and spoke to him about "things" that didn't really involve acting. Then Meyer casually said, "Okay, we're gonna go with you."

I said, "Yay!" And just like that, I had the best agent in town.

10. PLAY

Please Laugh At Yourself

I GOT A JOB ON THE TELEVISION SHOW *Kung Fu,* which was very popular in 1973. The show starred David Carradine and Chief Dan George. Because I was Native American myself (my grandma was half-blood Lenape Kansas Delaware), it was sacred to be on the set with Chief Dan George.

After filming ended for the day, I went to David's trailer, with the rest of the cast, to play guitar. We were smoking funny cigarettes, playing music, and having a great time. I got thirsty, so I asked David for some water to drink.

He pointed at a glass on the table. "There's grapefruit juice."

I chugged it down, then resumed playing the guitar. A little later, there was a knock on the door. It was the assistant director, who said, "We've decided to shoot the fight scene again in slow motion. We need you guys on set in thirty minutes."

We set our guitars down, put our 1800s period costumes back on, and went to the set. As I was walking, I noticed something strange happening with my saliva glands. It was so weird, I mentioned it to David. "There may have been Clearlight in the grapefruit juice," David casually mentioned. Clearlight is acid, a.k.a. LSD.

When I got to the set, I was tripping. My voice changed; it became slow, stilted, and lethargic. I was doing a scene with Chief Dan George, Billy Katt, and David Carradine. In the scene, I had to pour flour on Chief Dan's head, smash his wire-rimmed glasses with my foot, and make fun of him. Doing this to Chief Dan George while on acid made me very upset. He was one of my Native American heroes. While we waited for production to set up the shot, I sat down next to Chief Dan. He had his eyes closed while a young lady combed his long hair. I gushed, "Chief, I would never do this to you in real life. I have Native American blood, too. I'm so sorry about this."

A minute went by, then Chief Dan put his hand on my right thigh and laughed. "Don't worry. I know how to play the game."

As I peaked on acid, I got a great sense of relief from Chief Dan. It was as if I had tapped into the universal truth of humanity with his words. They sparked a revelation: "Life is a game to play." The acid didn't wear off until later that night, but honestly, it was a good trip.

11. FORGIVE

Finding Ourselves Really Giving
Individuals Valuable Energy

IN 1974, eight years after I moved to California, my parents came to visit for the first time. By then, I was making a decent amount of money acting, so I moved my family to a nice, middle-class home on Covello Street in Canoga Park. I knew Mom would be proud of what I had accomplished. Dad not so much. Nothing I did made Dad proud.

I had just been cast as a regular in a new comedy series produced by Mary Tyler Moore's production company, MTM Enterprises, called *The Texas Wheelers*. I played the oldest of three brothers being raised by their long-lost cranky father. With Dale McRaven—creator of *The Partridge Family* (and future creator of *Mork and Mindy*)—at the helm, starring veteran film actor (and hero of mine) Jack Elam playing my dad and a pre–Luke Skywalker Mark Hamill playing one of my brothers, the show had promise. We filmed on the CBS Radford lot in Studio City, right next door to *The Mary Tyler Moore Show,* which was at the height of its popularity. I was working nonstop on the show, so my parents visited me on the set. While they were there, we ran into Valerie Harper, who was filming on the stage next door. When I introduced Valerie to my parents, she touched Dad's shoulder and exclaimed with enthusiasm, "You are so handsome! Now I know where Gary gets his good looks." My dad turned bright red and flashed a massive smile aimed directly at me.

That was the first time in my life Dad ever smiled at me.

I had become so accustomed to his perpetual stone-cold scowl that I didn't know what to do with myself. I felt like I was two years old again, the same age when I met Dad for the first time.

He was just back from World War II at the time, and Mom introduced us. "Gary, this is your dad, Delmer Lloyd Busey." The large, imposing man was scowling as he looked down at me. I couldn't comprehend the scowl. I had never encountered anyone with such an expression. Mom and my two aunts Ruth and Sis, who had raised me thus far, were always so happy, doting on my every need with such love and affection.

I pointed at the man before me. "That's not my dad." Then I pointed to the picture on the wall of *my* dad, the man Mom had shown me every day of my two-year life with that comforting smile. "*That's* my dad."

"They're both your dad." Mom chuckled.

And it was settled—back to life with a new person in the house, but this new person looked scary.

Growing up, Dad brought a very militaristic way of being. His motto: "Children are to be seen and not heard." I had to ask his permission to speak. When I didn't, I was sent to my room. Dad demanded that everything be tidy, clothes hung up, dishes washed, bed made so tight you could bounce a coin on it, lights out at 8:30 P.M. (even through high school), and lots of discipline.

Around kindergarten, Dad began to discipline me physically. The physical discipline started with Dad washing my mouth out with soap. He found the biggest bar of black Lava soap he could and jammed it as far down my mouth as possible. Tears would spill out of my eyes, but I wasn't allowed to cry. "Crying is for sissy boys," Dad always repeated.

By the time I was in elementary school, Dad spanked me regularly. If I hadn't done something right, if I spoke back to my mom, if Dad didn't like the way I ate, if I did *anything* slightly out of line—I got disciplined. I became scared to death to even look in his face, because he might get me for just looking at him. "Take your pants down. Hold your ankles," he ordered in his deep, forbidding voice. Then he'd grab a belt, or a hanger, or a tree branch and swat me several times with it. There was never any warning when the spankings would come, but they happened so often I found a technique to put my mind far away from what he was doing, into an imagination zone, where nothing he did could hurt me.

Dad was tough. One time he grabbed a coat hanger to spank me, but the hook accidentally pierced all the way through his finger. His expression didn't change. With blood spurting everywhere, he casually yanked the hanger out, waltzed over to the sink, and ate Brazil nuts, cracking them open with blood dripping down his fingers. It was quite a sight.

Dad liked to barbecue with friends. They'd drink beer and tell war stories. One day while Dad was barbecuing, he told his best buddy Don Moon that he accidentally killed a young father, mother, and child in the war. Dad was inebriated, so he didn't realize my brother, David, was listening. When David told me what he heard, I saw Dad in a whole new light. It came to me Dad was still at war, right here in Tulsa, and I was his enemy. I became even more frightened of him.

I was twelve years old the first time Dad hugged me. After a night of drinking, he slipped into my room while I was sleeping. As I slept, he wrapped his arms around me, gushing, "I love you . . . I love you . . . I love you." It was the first time he'd ever said that to me. Then the hugs escalated; within seconds, he was squeezing me hard. He jerked me up and down, hitting me in the head with a pillow, shouting, "I love you! I love you!" My body was snapping in all different directions, slamming against the headboard. *Dad was beating me up.* My mother tried to pull him off, but she couldn't. With every ounce of strength I could muster, I pushed him hard and ran into the bathroom, screaming, "I hate you! I hate you! I hate you!" The words spilled out of my mouth. For the first time, I told him how I felt, and I meant every single word. In the bathroom, I took a deep, hard look at myself in the mirror. My nose was bleeding, my face pulverized. I felt terribly weak . . . like a loser; the furthest thing from a champion I could possibly be. As I cleaned myself up, I realized that this was a turning point in my life, because I could visualize everything I was going to go through with this man, my father, and I *accepted* the fact that this was who he was.

After that night, Dad never beat me up again—instead, he ignored me. When he came to my school plays or football games, his face was always expressionless. He never uttered one word of congratulations or support. Eventually

With my dad, Delmer Lloyd Busey.

I got used to his lack of sentiment toward me. But although I was used to it, deep down I still yearned for his acceptance, some type of positive reinforcement, a simple word of praise or congratulations for *anything* I achieved, big or small.

But that never came.

We did enjoy one thing together—watching television. Dad loved television. His favorite shows were *Gunsmoke* and *Hee Haw*. Television was the only thing we had in common besides football. When he came to California and watched me film *The Texas Wheelers,* he looked at me with expressions that said, "I'm so proud of you, Gary, for doing what you've done." His behavior toward me was different . . . he saw his firstborn son succeed in a field that was so far from his grasp of reality. During lunch, we went out to my van, where he asked me questions about what it was like in the entertainment business, making movies, making television shows. He spoke to me with such respect; he even gave me a real hug. I explained my experiences as best I could. After twenty-nine years, it felt good to finally have Dad express interest in something I had to say. It felt like a father and son reborn. Dad finally accepted me!

In 1975, Dad was diagnosed with a brain tumor. The tumor was a mass with fingers like an octopus. Doctors were able to remove the mass, but the fingers were inoperable. After the surgery, the doctor warned, "This will grow back in six weeks." Sure enough—to the day—the tumor grew back. Dad spent the next six weeks in the hospital, then died.

Sometime later, Mom told me, "You know what your dad said just before he died?"

"What?"

"He said, 'I wish I had it to do over again with Gary.'"

"Why didn't he tell me that?"

"He had too much Native American pride."

Having that special time with Dad on his visit to California was a blessing. I got to see him in a whole different light. Even though he never asked, I forgave him for what he did to me. I understood he was a victim of war, suffering from post-traumatic stress disorder after killing that family. I have always loved my dad. It was a tough upbringing, but I went through it; I made it. I want everyone to know that what I went through with my dad was very grueling, but it was meant to be. The difficulty I endured made me the man I am today with a strong, stable foundation. Plus, the militaristic family structure made me very punctual. I am never late.

The Texas Wheelers was canceled after four episodes. I was told the show didn't do well because there was too much conflict between the dad character and his sons. Another reason the show didn't do well was because it was broadcast against the hit show *The Rockford Files*.

12. DEATH

Don't Expect A Tragedy Here

B Y THE TIME I LANDED a guest spot on *Gunsmoke* in 1975, I already had over a dozen movie and television credits to my name. It was a real meaty part. After getting kicked in the head by a horse, my character suffers a brain injury—ironic, I know—and unknowingly has a week to live. The first scene I did was with Milburn Stone, who played Doc Adams. When the director said, "Action," I froze.

"Gary, you have the first line," the director reminded me.

"Oh!"

They reset. "Action."

I froze again.

"Gary, we're waiting for your line."

"Oh—uh!"

"Gary, is there anything wrong we can help you with?"

"No, I just . . . I've been watching this show all my life, and here I am with Doc in his office. It's just too . . ." I was speechless. I couldn't articulate what was going on with me. This show had started when I was in the fifth grade. I watched it every week with Dad. We never missed an episode. I felt like I knew each character personally. It was hard for me to fathom the reality of where I was—on that set in Doc's office—after watching it for so many years.

"Gary, you got the part playing the kid with the head injury. Go on and say the lines. *Action!*"

It took a moment, but I finally got my line out. After that, everything went fine. We shot the episode in five (long) twelve-hour days. In my last scene, my character finally succumbs to the brain injury and dies in Mitch Hansen's arms. This was the first time I'd ever died in a show. I researched head injuries and decided to die with my eyes crossed and open.

Shortly after the episode wrapped, maybe three days, I found out I had to go back to reshoot the ending because people weren't allowed to die on television with their eyes open. I went back and did it again with my eyes shut and got paid another day of work—no tragedy here. Not long after my episode of *Gunsmoke,* the show was canceled after eighteen years on the air, which gave me the honor of being the last guy to die on *Gunsmoke.*

13. ARTIST

A Real Tower In Seeking Truth

Between acting gigs, I went back home to Tulsa for a visit. One night while driving with friends, we turned into a church parking lot.

I laughed. "Are we going to a service?"

A friend replied, "Like one you've never seen before."

Inside, to my surprise, the church was swarming with lively happy partygoers.

"What is this place?" I asked.

"Leon Russell's Church Studio." The artistic ambience of the studio struck me right in the heart. The exotic lighting transported me to a remote tropical island. Leon's instruments were strewn about in such an expressive style of design, it made me want to play, sing, cry, and scream all at once. Everything I laid my eyes on gave my emotions a different color.

At the time, no one was recording or playing, so I slipped over to the drums, sat down, and played a soft beat. After a few minutes, a piano accompanied me. It was none other than *Leon Russell himself*! *The* Leon Russell, Tulsa icon, master songwriter and performer around the world! We played remarkably well *together*. Completely improvised, our collaboration was an incredible creative energy of artistic expression. It touched my heart deeply; it was by far the most magical musical experience of my life. "Teddy Jack, it's good to meet you," Leon said. I laughed. He thought I was Teddy Jack Eddy—a character I played on a local sketch comedy television show in Tulsa called *Mazeppa Pompazoidi's Uncanny Film Festival and Camp Meeting*. The character Teddy Jack Eddy had actually become semifamous locally in Tulsa. Most people, when they saw me on the street, thought I was Teddy Jack (not Gary Busey). Heck, sometimes I knew I was Teddy Jack Eddy, too.

"Good to meet you, too. My real name is Gary Busey. Teddy Jack is just the name of a character I play on TV." But to Leon, I *was* Teddy Jack. He continued to call me Teddy Jack as long as I knew him. Later, he would even name his firstborn son Teddy Jack after my character on the *Mazeppa* show and name me Teddy Jack's godfather.

After my first meeting with Leon, I went back to LA, where I had a big boom in my acting career. Months passed before I had the time to visit Leon again. The first chance I got, I went back to Tulsa to see him, this time at his estate, where he had recently relocated his studio. I had just mastered a drumbeat no one had heard before, based on something I learned in the tenth grade: "the ham bone." I blasted my new ham bone drum riff for Leon. It was a powerhouse rhythm with so many different beats happening all at the same time. Like an eighteen-wheeler going 250 miles an hour straight into your heart.

With Leon Russell at the Tulsa State Fair in 1973.
*(Photo by Steve Todoroff. Courtesy of the Oklahoma
Historical Society OKPOP Collections.)*

Going anywhere with Leon Russell.
(*Courtesy of Dan Mayo*)

"Whoa, Teddy Jack. That sounded like three drummers. Where did you learn to play that?" Leon asked.

"I'm self-taught." Then I did the ham bone for Leon, on my body. It made him laugh.

"I never heard anything like that. Let's record some music, you on drums, me on piano," Leon suggested.

"Sure."

For the first time, I recorded music with Leon Russell. He was on a different level from any artist I had ever met. He worked quietly without effort, never pushing, always remaining calm, cool, and collected, mixing just the right instruments to make a colorful array of musical visions no one had ever heard before. I left the studio that day exhilarated, feeling as though I had become a better artist just for having been in Leon's presence.

After that incredible visit, Leon's wife, Mary, called me often. "Leon would like you to come over to play drums."

I'd say, "Yay!" and skedaddle over there as fast as possible.

Pretty soon, Leon asked, "How much do you make in a week?"

"Three thousand."

"I can pay you five hundred, plus room and board, to play with me."

"Okay." Judy, Jake, and I moved into Leon's estate in Tulsa for the next few months while I worked with Leon on his latest album, *Will O' the Wisp*. It was a miracle and blessing to sit with Leon in the control room, arranging music.

One day while we were working, Leon played me a song he wrote, then asked, "What do you visualize when you hear this?"

His song was so expressive, a vision came to me instantly: "A man and woman on camels at the top of a sand dune during sunset, discovering a spring that never stops running, which becomes their little hideaway."

In no time, Leon lyricized the song he called "Little Hideaway." It blew my mind. Making music was so easy for Leon. I wanted to know his secret. I asked, "Leon, how do you do this? What's your method here?"

"I don't have a method."

"Are you just out there on your own?"

"I'm not on my own, but I'm out there."

He put the *Will O' the Wisp* album together perfectly. I had the privilege of playing drums on three cuts, "Blue

Bird," "Little Hideaway," and "Make You Feel Good," under the pseudonym Teddy Jack Eddy (which later earned me a gold record).

Even after working with him and watching him very closely, I still couldn't figure out his magic. Then I had an epiphany. Leon never thought about what he was doing; it always came naturally from his heart. Sometimes he stayed in bed for four weeks waiting for the next creative journey to come. Everything he did, from staying in bed to creating an ambience that helped him write music, was his way of finding the truth of his heart.

Working with Leon during those extremely informative years helped me become the artist I am today. When Leon Russell passed away, I felt as if a part of me went with him, but then there is part of him that is still here with me in my heart.

14. MUSIC

Magnificent **U**nique **S**ound
Inviting **C**reativity

WHEN LEON RUSSELL TOLD ME I was going on the road with him to play drums for his *Will O' the Wisp* tour, it was as if all my musical dreams were coming true. Leon didn't give me a choice; he said, "Gary, we're going on the road," and I said, "Okay!"

Leaving Judy and Jake behind for a few months didn't concern me at all—I had just moved them into a nice house in a safe neighborhood in a suburb of Los Angeles called the San Fernando Valley. Plus, she knew from the start she was marrying a music man. When I left for the road, Judy seemed happy for me.

"This is a long way from the Rubber Band," she reflected.

"It sure is."

"I know how important it is for you to play drums with Leon. Have a great time."

"I will. I'll see you in three months." I kissed Judy and Jake, then grabbed my bag—stuffed with Hawaiian shirts, Levi's, and sneakers—and hit the road.

She shouted after me, "We'll be here when you get back!"

We toured on two Continental buses—one for Leon, his wife, Mary, and a few roadies; the other for the band and backup singers. Each bus, singularly designed by Leon, was equipped with beds, bathrooms, and a galley. I chose to sleep in the first bunk right in front—easy on, easy off. At first, being on a bus going down the highways and byways of life from one venue to another sounded fun, but once we got on the road, I had a harsh awakening. I was claustrophobic. I also had not anticipated all the downtime on the road; I got very impatient. Not only was I claustrophobic and impatient, I also felt out of my element. Life on the road was a happening I had no control of. It was follow the leader. Luckily, the leader was Leon Russell. I followed his every move, I paid attention thirty hours a day just to make sure I was okay, in the right line, hitting the right spot in the right light to hit the right beat.

Eventually, even though I was overwhelmed mentally, physically, emotionally, and spiritually, I began to see the foundation that life on the road was giving me. I started to feel like I belonged on the road. The more the band toured together, the closer we became—like a tribe. Our time on the bus was a constant rehearsal. The lead guitarist always played from his bunk, which gave us all the opportunity to practice our harmonies. I even started writing my own songs. In fact, one practically wrote itself, called "I'm Still in Love with You." It was for Judy; I really missed her.

One thing I could not acclimate to was not having a shower. I got so desperate to get clean, one day when the bus pulled into a filling station in Monroe, Louisiana, I noticed a coin-operated self-serve car wash. "Let's take a shower!" I proclaimed as I ran off the bus, stripped-down naked in broad daylight. It was the best—*and only*—shower I had until I got back home.

The venues we played were huge ballrooms, stadiums, and amphitheaters, crowded with thousands of people. This was the big time—nothing like the little bars my four-piece band had played. At one particular stadium in Charlotte, North Carolina, the acoustics were so incredible, I swear I could hear each note from every instrument, each voice from every backup singer, and Leon and Mary as clear as crystal water. It was all very intoxicating. I had no idea music could go so deep inside of me the way it did. After each show, the excitement stayed with me for hours. I felt so big for playing two and a half hours of music to people screaming for more. It took a while to come down. Some of the guys had groupies to help them come down, but since I was married, that wasn't an option.

On the road, I experimented with drugs (mostly marijuana and a little cocaine). Right before one show at the Avalon Theatre in Chicago, I went to the bathroom, where I ran into some guy I'd never met before. "Hey, you want some of mine?" he asked, motioning to some powder that looked like cocaine.

Like a nine-year-old child who wants to try everything, I said, "Sure." Without asking this stranger exactly what I was about to put in my body, I snorted away. I had an immediate reaction. *A very strange reaction.* A feeling in my gut told me, *Uh-oh. This is not what you thought it was.*

"What is this?" I asked the stranger in a panic.

"PCP."

"Is that like coke?"

"Better than coke." He reminded me of a devil's disciple.

Rubberleggin' with the Leon Russell Show.
(*Courtesy of Steve Todoroff*)

The feelings I went through on PCP were not my own, although they came from me. I was floating with nowhere to go—and no way to return. It was very frightening. I got the feeling that snakes were slowly wriggling throughout every part of my body. Anxiety set in. My heart pounded faster than any beat I could ever drum. I knew I had nailed myself viciously to the wall of no return, but somehow, I managed to get myself onstage. I could barely move, let alone play the drums. At one point during the show, I was supposed to go to the center of the stage, dance the rubber leg, take my cowboy hat off, spin it up in the air where it would land right back on my head, then dirty bop over to Leon at the piano, then bop my way back to the drums and continue playing. The audience always went nuts when I

BUSEYISMS

did this, but that night, I locked up. I couldn't move. All of a sudden, a pack of Marlboro cigarettes whizzed past my head. It was Leon; he threw them at me to remind me that I'd missed my cue. I staggered to the middle of the stage and stumbled through my jig. With the grace of God, I managed to get through the whole show.

When the show ended, Leon asked, "Do you need to go to the hospital?"

"No." Intuitively, I knew I could overcome this on my own. Leon took me to a hotel where, for the first time on our tour, I got a room. I came down from PCP in my hotel room watching the new movie *Taxi Driver*. The next morning, I was fine.

Before we set out for the road again, Leon asked, "You ready to play?"

"Yes, sir."

"Okay, let's go." We got on the bus and took off for our next venue.

The three months I spent on the road with Leon created a sense of maturity in me that I'd never had. It was advanced learning in a music class I never expected to receive. I learned I was good enough to play in professional shows, with professional musicians, in big arenas. When the tour ended, I felt a pang of withdrawal before I even got home.

I arrived home on Thanksgiving of all days. Since I didn't have a chance to call Judy from the road, I decided to surprise her. Happy and battered from my adventure, I quietly tiptoed to the door and slid my key in the lock, but it didn't work. I knocked.

Judy opened the door a crack. "You can't come inside."

"Why not?"

"I haven't heard from you in three months."

With Leon Russell.
(*Courtesy of Steve Todoroff*)

It hadn't even occurred to me to call her. I guess I felt she would understand that I was on a bus across the country doing professional shows, not stopping to use pay phones. That was my logical thinking at the time, which now I know wasn't logical at all. I could argue this was before cell phones, but the truth is I just didn't have all the ingredients needed to be a proper husband yet. What I did have, though, was music. I grabbed my acoustic guitar. "I wrote a song for you." With the door between us, I serenaded Judy with the song I wrote for her, "I'm Still in Love with You." Slowly, with tears in her eyes, she smiled, opened the door, and gave me a delicious hug. In that moment, I learned that music is love, and love is music. Music is truly the highest art form of all that can make miracles happen.

With all that I am, I thank you and I love you, Leon.

The Gumball Rally, 1976. (Licensed by Warner Bros. Entertainment, Inc. All Rights Reserved.)

15. TRUTH

Taking Real Understanding To Heart

I WAS IN THE MIDDLE of filming a movie called *The Gumball Rally* when I heard Barbra Streisand and her coproducer/hairdresser/boyfriend Jon Peters wanted to meet me about a movie called *A Star Is Born* for the part of a rock-and-roll road manager named Bobbie Ritchie. I went to Warner Bros., excited to meet this incredible, mega-powerful icon Barbra Streisand. The big surprise I got when we met was the feeling that she was just as excited to meet me. Barbra welcomed me with gracious eyes of acceptance. She genuinely seemed interested to get to know me, asking questions rapid fire.

"Have you seen Polly Platt?" (She was referring to Polly Platt in the wardrobe department.)

"No."

"Who dressed you?"

"I did."

"Is this how you normally dress?"

"Yes."

The excited look on Barbra's face gave me the impression that I'd struck her as visually perfect for the part. I wore a bandanna around my neck, a long-sleeved red shirt with a short-sleeved Hawaiian shirt layered on top, jeans, and cowboy boots.

"What do you do?" she continued.

"I'm playing drums with Leon Russell."

"You know Leon? How can we meet him?"

Minutes later, Barbra and Jon were in my van on their way to meet Leon, who had recently moved to California.

"Nice ride," Barbra said. She was taking in the details of my van—customized to emulate a ship—with nautical seagoing art throughout, a steering wheel with eight handles like the wheel of a ship, and a CB radio.

"It's my pirate ship." Out of the corner of my eye, I noticed Barbra staring at me. I had no idea what she was thinking.

We drove the thirty minutes from Warner Bros. to Leon's house on Woodley Avenue in Encino discussing whatever came to mind like we all were old friends.

Since Leon and I were together every day playing music, he was expecting me sometime after my meeting. I decided to surprise him with Barbra. When Leon opened the door and saw us, he casually said, "Teddy Jack, whatcha got here?" Leon never gave away any emotions in his face or his behavior.

"I'd like you to meet my new friends, Barbra Streisand and Jon Peters."

We went inside and talked about *A Star Is Born*. Barbra complimented Leon's music. Then, right there in Leon's house, Barbra sang a duet with Leon's wife, Mary, to a song Leon wrote called "This Masquerade." Their two voices with Leon's piano sounded heavenly. It was a great new

A Star Is Born, 1976, wearing the same clothes I wore at my audition.
(Licensed by Warner Bros. Entertainment, Inc. All Rights Reserved.)

A Star Is Born, 1976, with Barbra Streisand.
(Licensed by Warner Bros. Entertainment, Inc. All Rights Reserved.)

union. Because of our afternoon together, Leon ended up with his song "Lost Inside of You" in the movie, and I got the part.

With one week left on *The Gumball Rally,* I had to do double duty: days on *A Star Is Born* in Beverly Hills, and nights on *Gumball Rally* in Long Beach at the Queen Mary . . . sleep—not much.

During the filming of *A Star Is Born,* it was apparent that Barbra was the captain of this airplane. Very hands-on, she had a knack for capturing the truth in every moment of every scene, constantly offering me great suggestions on how I could enhance my part. I took her suggestions to heart but ultimately drew on *my* truth. I played my part the way a road manager would, based on my experience playing rock and roll, dealing with road managers. Sometimes my way was different from Barbra's vision, but the end result was exactly what the movie needed: truth.

One day when we came out from watching the dailies, Barbra said, "Busey, now I know what to do to make you do it my way."

"What's that?"

"Tell you the opposite."

I laughed. "Close . . . but no guitar." Then it dawned on me—maybe she had been telling me the opposite all along? She was a brilliant sister of cocreating the truth.

A Star Is Born, 1976, with Kris Kristofferson.
(Licensed by Warner Bros. Entertainment, Inc. All Rights Reserved.)

16. CHILD

Candid Honesty In Loving Doses

I MMEDIATELY AFTER I WRAPPED *A Star Is Born*, I got word that Dustin Hoffman wanted to meet me about the part of a heroin-addicted bank robber in the movie *Straight Time*. In the meeting with Dustin, he didn't talk much, but when he did, it was always about the character, the movie, or how I felt about this or that. He studied me with intensity, watching my every reaction, as we discussed the nuances of the character Willy Darin. I had already been to multiple Narcotics Anonymous meetings while preparing for a television show I did called *Baretta* with Strother Martin, Mackenzie Phillips, and Robert Blake, so instinctively, I already knew who this character was. After a few meetings, I was very honored to find out that Dustin chose me for the part.

Once I was cast, Dustin told me he needed a young actor to play my son. Over the few weeks I spent getting to know Dustin during the casting process, Dustin had become acquainted with my five-year-old son, Jake. He thought Jake was perfect for the part and suggested Jake come in for a screen test.

Excited about the prospect, Judy and I took Jake to the Holiday Inn hotel on Sunset Boulevard by the 405 Freeway in Brentwood to meet with Dustin and the *Straight Time* casting director. They had the hotel room set up like a casting office with a folding table, chairs, and a camera. There was only one other boy at the screen test. He was probably around ten years old with dark hair—obviously meant to look like Kathy Bates, my on-screen wife. The casting director took both boys in the room together to meet Dustin. After about ten minutes, the older boy was dismissed, but Jake remained in the room. We waited another ten minutes on pins and needles before Jake emerged with a slight grin on his precious little face. Judy and I were so excited we bombarded him with rapid-fire questions: "What happened? How did you like it? Tell us everything!"

Jake was cool as a cucumber. He didn't offer a lot of details. "We played with a wooden duck."

"Then what?" I asked.

"He asked questions."

"What kind of questions?"

"How old am I . . . what do I like to do . . . my favorite color . . . can I ride a bike . . ."

"What did you say?"

"I told him I like drumming."

I'd been teaching Jake the drums ever since he could hold drumsticks. At five, he was already a great drummer.

"Do you want to be in the movie?" we asked.

"Of course, that's why I'm here."

It didn't take long after the audition to find out that Jake got the part. Dustin said he was a natural—so at age five,

Straight Time, 1978, with my son Jake Busey, Dustin Hoffman, and Kathy Bates. *(Licensed by Warner Bros. Entertainment, Inc. All Rights Reserved.)*

Jake landed his first movie role, opposite Dustin Hoffman, Kathy Bates, and yours truly. We took Jake to meet my agent, Meyer Mishkin, to handle the deal. While I chatted with Meyer, Jake sat on the floor playing with a see-through plastic piggy bank with five levels for each type of coin—silver dollar, quarter, dime, nickel, and penny. I gave Jake a handful of pennies to add to his bank. He carefully put each penny in, one at a time, watching them drop. Then he dumped the pennies out and counted them.

While Jake worked on his pennies, Meyer congratulated him. "Jake, you're going to be in your first motion picture. How do you feel about it?"

"I'm happy."

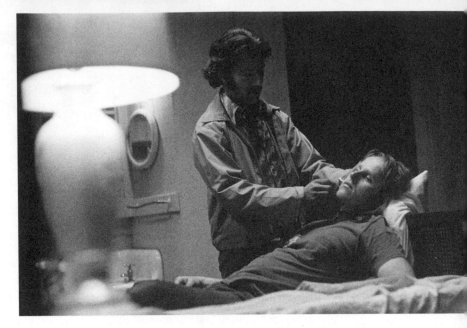

Straight Time, 1978, with Dustin Hoffman. *(Licensed by Warner Bros. Entertainment, Inc. All Rights Reserved.)*

"Let me ask you something very important. How much money do you want to get paid for acting in this movie?"

Jake thought very carefully, then said, "Well, I have 159 pennies, so I want 159 dollars, 159 quarters, 159 dimes, and 159 nickels." He was so cute when he said that he melted all of our hearts.

"I think we can do that!" Meyer chortled.

Jake got to pick the name of his character for the movie. At the time, he was going through a phase where he wanted to change his name to Henry—he even had the kids in his kindergarten class calling him Henry—so naturally that's the name he chose for his character. Jake had three days of work on the movie. He went through each scene like a little pro. Between scenes, Jake drew. He always carried an art box equipped with everything you could possibly need to draw: colored pencils, markers, crayons, rulers, you name it. He was obsessed with drawing semitrucks.

On Jake's last day of work, he had his biggest scene with Kathy Bates, Dustin, and me in the dining room. After we rehearsed, the lighting took an especially long time to set up. When we were finally ready to go, we brought Jake to the set.

Jake casually announced, "I'm only doing this one time."

"Why?" we asked.

"I want to draw trucks." What could we say? He did the scene only one time, as he said he would—and nailed it.

On our way home, I told Jake (who was still drawing trucks), "You did great."

"I know."

"What do you think about acting now?"

"I think it's the dumbest thing I've ever done."

"Why?"

"Because all you do is pretend, but you play like you're not pretending, and I'd rather be drawing trucks."

(From left to right) George Greenough, Greg MacGillivray, John Milius, Gary Busey, Dan Merkel, William Katt, and Jan-Michael Vincent.

17. SURF

Standing Up Riding Free

WHILE I WAS DOING *Straight Time* on the Warner Bros. lot, word was getting out about me in the industry. I had become the hot new guy—a force of nature with lots of energy, lots of teeth, lots of fluffy blond hair, and a very truthful style of acting. I caught the attention of writer-director John Milius. John was an amazing filmmaker who came out of USC film school in the same class with George Lucas. He wanted to meet me about a surf movie he was doing called *Big Wednesday*.

The one thing I remember most about our first meeting is that I made John laugh hysterically all the time, just by being me. Even before he told me about the movie, I knew I had the part just by how much I made him laugh. We were both kindred spirits—assertive, gregarious, forceful, and funny. He told me about the character he had in mind for me: a California surfer coming of age during the Vietnam War era, named Leroy, a.k.a. "the Masochist." The Masochist, a guy who liked pain and the sight of blood, could dive through windows, drink cups of vomit, and eat light-bulbs. I told John, "No acting required here."

"Do you surf?"

"There's no surfing in Texas or Oklahoma."

"Well, we got to go out and see how you do."

John, an avid teenage surfer in the '60s, took me to one of his favorite surf spots in Malibu, Surfrider Beach. Having a deep fascination with the military, John looked at surfing like warfare: "The waves are dragons . . . the surfers are knights . . . and the surfboards are lances." First, John taught me how to stand on the board in the sand. Once I got the hang of getting up quickly in the sand, he put me in the water with a nine-foot-six-inch board. "When you feel the back end of the board raise, quickly stand up like you did in the sand, and surf!" he commanded.

"Okay." A wave about three feet high came. I stood up quickly and rode it for about ninety feet. I couldn't believe how easy it was. John had a wide-eyed, openmouthed look of shocked excitement on his face. I asked him, "Is that it? Is that all there is to it?"

"You never surfed before?"

"No, I'm from Texas and Oklahoma. I played football; that's a collision sport. I could snap your sternum and loosen your teeth. This surfing is for sissy boys."

I got the part.

Jan-Michael Vincent and I left for Maui to study surfing with John's favorite surfer, Gerry Lopez. Jan already knew how to surf, but I knew nothing. I had one month to learn. I immersed myself in the surfing culture, replacing *The Hollywood Reporter* and *Variety* with surf magazines. Gerry Lopez, known as Mr. Pipeline for being the best tube rider in the world (and winner of the Pipeline Masters competition in

Big Wednesday, 1978, with Jan-Michael Vincent and William Katt.
(Licensed by Warner Bros. Entertainment, Inc. All Rights Reserved.)

1972 and 1973), was on all the covers. He was about five foot eight, half-Cuban, half-Japanese, with a calm, cool, laid back, harmonious, ocean-warrior disposition. He started out by telling me that surfing was a proper gesture of Zen, with no thinking, no understanding, and no figuring anything out. "Just let nature take you on an amazing ride." It was as if Gerry spoke a special language called "Ocean." He could see how the waves were breaking onto the shore and understand exactly what was happening at the bottom of the ocean to create waves in different places along the coast. From Gerry's house, he could deduce how big the waves were all the way across the island, at his favorite surfing spot, Honolua Bay.

During the month I lived at Gerry's house, I slept on the floor. Every morning, I woke up to Gerry's Hoover vacuum cleaner at my feet and crotch. Our daily routine: coffee and oatmeal, run a mile and a half on the sand, swim in the ocean for an hour and a half, shower on the beach, surf for four hours. We finished the day off at Kimo's restaurant and ate clam chowder with a big piece of chocolate cake, followed by some Maui Wowie. It was a great time. I knew the universe had given me a tremendous gift to live with and be trained by Gerry Lopez in an amazing new sport of surfing.

Gerry gradually worked me up to surfing the big waves. When he felt I was good enough, he brought me into twenty-five-foot waves. He also taught me how to wipe out. "When a strong wave holds you down underwater and you can't come up to the surface, *don't fight it*. Turn yourself into a dishrag and imagine you're being dried in a drying machine." There were times I wiped out in twenty-five-foot surf that kept me underwater for minutes. It was downright scary, but I kept doing what Gerry instructed with *no thinking* about it. Soon I enjoyed the wipeouts. My nickname became Scary Gary because I would go out in huge swells, wipe out, then pop my head out of the water hollering, "Yay! Let's do it again!" I was ready to go.

We shot most of the movie in California. John Milius was like a brigadier general, and I was his lieutenant. It felt like he had several ranks over me. With confidence, he gave me orders, and I followed through exactly as instructed. His directions opened new ideas for me that hadn't crossed my mind. When I had a problem with any of the lines, John always enlightened me. One particular line really stumped me—"Surfboards, women, and guns"—so I asked John, "What's the motivation?"

He said with passion, "You're talking about the three best things in the world." John had a way of making my artistic lightbulb shine as brightly as possible. He also gave me free rein to be me. He said, "You *are* the Masochist. Just go and do what you do."

For the final sequence, we moved to Sunset Beach on the North Shore of Oahu at the height of big-wave season. Four months had passed since I'd caught that three-foot wave with John at Surfrider Beach. The waves at Sunset Beach were the biggest I'd ever seen. Two words came out of my mouth without thought: *"Jesus—palomino!"* The first wave I caught was thirty feet; I rode it all the way. It was so scary and exciting I didn't know what I was feeling.

Afterward, I went to John. "I got something to tell you."

"What's that?"

"Surfing is *not* for sissy boys."

John gave me a sturdy pat on the back. "I knew you would learn. You just had to come out here and taste those dragons."

With John Milius, 2015. *(Courtesy of Steffanie Sampson)*

18. MIRACLE

Moving **I**nto **R**apturous **A**ngelic
Cosmic **L**oving **E**nergy

W HILE I WAS IN THE MIDDLE OF FILMING *Big Wednesday,* I got a call from my agent, Meyer. "You have a
meeting at the Comstock Hotel on Wilshire for the movie
The Buddy Holly Story. You're going to meet the director
and the producers for the lead role."

"You mean for the role of Buddy Holly?"

"Yes."

"Oh God, okay." I had a hard time picturing it. Currently
in the middle of a surfing movie, I was a bulked-up, bronzed,
blond buck—the antithesis of the skinny, curly- and dark-
haired Buddy Holly with glasses. "Why are they seeing me?
Buddy was twenty-two when he died . . . I'm thirty-four. It
would take a miracle for me to get this part. I don't want to
go."

"Miracles happen every day. Might I remind you that
you're playing twenties right now in *Big Wednesday?*"

Besides the fact that Buddy Holly was my childhood hero
(*and* everyone in town had already been seen for this role),
it didn't feel truthful to the measurement of my power at

the time. I was still on my way up the ladder. A *lead role*? I'd never done that before. That was something you come up slowly on, make sure you don't rush it.

I told Meyer, "I'm not ready yet."

Meyer snapped, "They want to meet you, so you'll go tomorrow before you film, and that's that."

My mind wandered to the great Joyce Selznick with the perpetual glowing light all around her. Joyce was responsible for discovering Tony Curtis, George C. Scott, Kurt Russell, Faye Dunaway, Candice Bergen, and many more. I knew she was behind this meeting, force-feeding me to the producers. Since Joyce had cast me in *The Last American Hero* opposite Jeff Bridges five years earlier, she'd had an attraction to my spirit. Impressed with my talent, she offered to help me in the business. Not only had she become a mentor, she became a friend. I felt like I was Joyce's flower and she was going to water me, let the sun shine on me, and watch me grow. For some reason, Joyce had it in her heart that I was going to be Buddy Holly. She teased over and over, "You're going to be Buddy Holly! You're going to be Buddy Holly!"

The first Buddy Holly song I ever heard was "That'll Be the Day." I couldn't believe how good it was in every way. It was emotionally charging, and spiritually enlightening. The lyrics were funny, and the song had a beat you *had* to dance to. Buddy's music was like nothing anyone had ever heard. It was like me—energetic and free. It flipped the generation over like a pancake because there were no more rules. When I found out he died, a big swell of emptiness enveloped me. I was in the ninth grade coming home from school at 3:30 P.M. that overcast day on February 3, 1959. I entered the living room of my house in Tulsa, Oklahoma, and heard a grave voice on the big mahogany radio announcing the deaths of Buddy Holly, Ritchie Valens, and J. P. "the Big Bopper" Richardson in a plane crash. I placed my binder on our modern 1959 coffee table and sank into the couch. I realized the music was gone. All the air seeped out of my body knowing there would never be anyone like Buddy Holly again.

The Last American Hero.
(© 1973 Twentieth Century Fox.
All Rights Reserved.)

As Meyer instructed, I met with the producers the next day. I was surprised to find out they were green-boned rookies and this was going to be their first film. They told me stories about Buddy Holly that were completely wrong. Three years earlier, I had been cast to play J. I. Allison—the drummer for Buddy Holly and the Crickets—in a movie called *Not Fade Away.* In preparation for that movie, I had the honor of spending time with the real J. I. Allison, who was also Buddy Holly's best friend. He told me stories about Buddy and the band and their time as kids growing up in Lubbock, Texas. But *Not Fade Away* got canned, I was told, because production did not have the money to secure the rights. I didn't know at the time that *Not Fade Away* was preparing me for this moment in this hotel room with this group of rookies who wanted to tell the true story about a young Texan guy who cofounded rock and roll and his tragic untimely death. I told the producers what I knew from meeting J. I. Allison. They were open and receptive to the truth. I got a feeling these guys were really gonna do their best to make a good movie.

After twenty minutes, I had to excuse myself. "I'm doing a surfing movie right now. I've got to ride some waves. Great to meet you guys, and good luck on your movie." I didn't give the meeting another thought.

Meyer called me right after the meeting. "They want to hear you sing Buddy Holly songs tomorrow at Village Recorders. They're going to record you because they plan on doing the songs live in the movie."

"Live? There'll never be anyone that can sing like Buddy Holly. Period. That's out of the question."

"Go!" Meyer barked.

I showed up with my guitar at Village Recorders. I didn't think the meeting was important at all until I noticed thirty people in the control room, with Joyce Selznick beaming right smack in the middle. They didn't have any lyrics for me to sing, and I didn't have any memorized, but since I knew the chords to some of Buddy's songs, I sang what few words I knew and made up the rest. After I did two songs, enough for them to hear my voice and see how I sang, I left.

The next day, Meyer called. "Congratulations! *You* are going to be *Buddy Holly*."

I felt the sky open up and lightning strike me with a bolt of energy as he uttered every word. It was an indescribable, ethereal feeling I'd never felt before that happened quicker than time could be measured on earth. I could not believe the honor bestowed upon me. I was going to portray an icon that had been alive, on earth, at the same time as I was. It was truly a miracle guided by forces greater than I was, pushing me in a direction I never imagined I could go, making me do things I never imagined I could do. I recalled how my life had been a series of miracles in a sequence of changes that had always come without effort. All I ever had to do was show up, be myself, do my best, and allow the forces around me to guide my instincts. I accepted this miracle and vowed to honor every aspect of Buddy's spirit and truth. *I was going to be Buddy Holly.*

19. NUTS

Never Underestimate The Spirit

I WAS SET TO START *The Buddy Holly Story* as soon as *Big Wednesday* wrapped. The funny thing was that we couldn't say exactly when that would be. We were at the North Shore in Oahu filming the ending, but everything depended on Mother Nature giving us twenty- to thirty-foot waves to represent the "Great Swell of '74" for our final shot. As it turned out, Mother Nature did not care about my schedule or that I had another movie to make; she took her good sweet time. We waited and waited, longer than expected. *The Buddy Holly Story* people called me. "Gary, what's taking so long?"

"We're waiting for a big wave."

"What? A wave? When is that going to happen?"

"Depends." I had no answer for them. Luckily, two days later—on a Wednesday—my *Big Wednesday* costar Billy Katt came running down the hallway of our hotel, shouting, "Busey! Busey! It's fifteen feet and rising at Sunset Beach!"

I immediately called the *Buddy Holly* people to let them know, "The big wave is here! Get ready to rock and roll!"

There are a handful of times when the stars align during the making of a movie and everything seems to fall into place perfectly, as if guided by angels—*The Buddy Holly Story* was one of them. After completing *Big Wednesday,* I arrived back in Los Angeles to find my itinerary and call sheet for *The Buddy Holly Story* waiting for me at home. I knew by the look of the itinerary and call sheet that although the filmmakers were green, I was going to be in very good hands. I switched gears from surf to rock and roll. There was no time for preparation, which was probably a good thing, because when you sit down and *think* about what you're going to do, you just get in the way of spontaneity. Production quickly transformed me into Buddy Holly. They dyed my hair black, gave it three permanents to make it curly, dressed me in stylish sharp clothes from the '50s, then crowned the whole look with Buddy Holly's very own authentic funny glasses. I couldn't find Gary Busey in the mirror. When I went onto the set and picked up the guitar for the first time, Gary Busey was gone.

Buddy always said, "Never compromise your music, and always make it danceable," so that became my motto for how I approached every scene. I was committed 150 percent to playing the part authentically. A lot of people think acting is saying the lines outwardly, but they are wrong. You have to start from within. Everything comes from within first; if you don't have it in you, it won't come out of you. I knew I could not do an impersonation of Buddy, because that would never work. I had to be completely truthful to him—how he really looked, sounded, moved, sang, walked, talked . . . his hand movements, his eye movements, the way

A personal photo off the set during the filming of *The Buddy Holly Story.*

he used his glasses, his hair, his clothes, the movement on-stage, the movement offstage. I considered everything about him. I always wore his glasses, even at home, because I needed those indentations on my nose, and it made me feel like Buddy. They never came off. I took Buddy with me everywhere I went.

The first scene we shot was a musical number where we played "Mockingbird Hill" in a roller rink, followed by "Ollie Vee." Since I didn't have time to memorize "Mockingbird Hill," I taped the lyrics to the top of my acoustic guitar and sang just like Buddy did, as if it were no big deal.

But it *was* a big deal. As the words came out of my mouth, I started to feel different . . . bigger. The excitement of the first shot actually overwhelmed me. What surprised me the most was how effortless and automatic it was for me to be Buddy Holly.

The pace of the production was so rapid it was like entering a time warp. Every day I went to work, it felt like I had stepped onto a speeding train, gaining momentum with every scene, whizzing through time and space, all the way to rock-and-roll heaven. We shot in sequence, twenty-three locations out of the studio, with almost every scene done in one take. We were all like hamsters spinning on the same wheel, with nobody hitting each other. Because of director Steve Rash's gentle force of nature, he gave us the ability to be precisely in the zone, with no pressure. His impeccable timing to speak with me before each shot gave me an ease that gave birth to my artistic freedom.

As we got deeper into the filming of the movie, everything continued to come naturally—*too* naturally. I didn't worry, plan, or think; nothing came up to distract me. I noticed there was definitely something *more* going on than just an actor portraying a part, something beyond me, something not from this earth. I began to perceive that I was being supported by a heaven of artistic angels, with Buddy Holly at the helm. In fact, I knew his spirit was with me. Especially when I sang his songs—I did the singing, it was my voice coming out, but it wasn't really me singing; it was Buddy. Buddy's spirit sang the songs through me. When you watch the movie, you'll see it in all the music; I was in a trance. The last scene in the movie when Buddy sang "True Love Ways," I was nowhere near the human zone; I was in a self-hypnotic space. When I finished the song, I turned around and said, "That made my heartbeat skip, y'all." That line wasn't in the script, but that was what Buddy Holly would have said, and he said it through me.

The last day of filming was on December 30, 1978, which also happened to be my tenth wedding anniversary. After the movie wrapped, I felt myself change, a release happened like colors leaving my body. It wasn't really quick like unplugging something; it was slow and easy. When I got home, Judy greeted me at the front door, all dolled up and looking very sexy. I walked over to her but stopped at the front door and asked, "Do I look different?"

She stood back to take a good look at me, then said, "Yeah, you do."

"Well, I feel different."

"How?"

"I feel lighter. I don't feel as big as I did when I was doing the movie, and the feelings I had when I was playing the part are gone."

"Welcome home." Judy gave me a kiss, then led me inside to a beautiful candlelit dinner celebration. It felt warm and relaxing, like a hot air balloon landing in the comfort of a beautiful meadow.

The Buddy Holly Story was a once-in-a-lifetime movie experience. To this day, I still feel deeply connected to Buddy. When I sing his songs, they're mine; I feel an ownership of them—not legally but spiritually. Getting to play the part, do the movie, sing the songs, was like a rite of passage for my heart and spirit, and that's the truth.

20. AWESOME

A Wonderful Experience Showing Others Magnificent Energy

AFTER *THE BUDDY HOLLY STORY* WRAPPED, I asked the director, Steve Rash, and the producer, Freddie Bauer, to set up a meeting with the Holley family. It took a couple of months, but soon I found myself in their modest middle-class family home in Lubbock, Texas, in the presence of Buddy's parents and siblings.

This was sacred ground.

Buddy's family gave me a friendly greeting and a Coca-Cola, and showed me around. The living room was a shrine to Buddy, with every single record he ever made still in the unopened cellophane displayed in stands (each one individually visible) . . . the LPs, the 45s, you name it. Four of his guitars—the very guitars that he played and wrote on—were right there in front of me. *Deep breath.* I picked up a guitar, in pristine condition, and played "Not Fade Away."

"Sounds just like Buddy," Mrs. Holley said. Then I got chills again—Buddy's spirit was back; I felt him again, right there with us.

I asked Mrs. Holley, "What was Buddy like when he was around writing songs?"

Mrs. Holley told me a story of her and Buddy. She said, "One day I asked him why he wrote songs like 'Peggy Sue, Peggy Sue, oh, pretty, pretty Peggy Sue.' And Buddy said, 'All I'm doing is writing nursery rhymes.'" Then Mrs. Holley told him, "Buddy, it's time for you to write a love song." She handed him the lyrics to a song she wrote, and Buddy put it to music. It became his first love song, "Maybe Baby."

Hearing about Buddy from his mother's point of view, firsthand, was too much to handle. She was simple, hospitable, loving, and eager to learn about how it felt for me to portray her son, Charles Hardin Holley—Buddy's real name. I told her it meant the world to me, and I meant every word. When I left the Holley home, Mrs. Holley said, "You're part of the Holley family now." Buddy's family treated me with such acceptance that I really felt like one of them.

The day before *The Buddy Holly Story* premiered at the Cinerama Dome in Hollywood (now called the ArcLight), I drove to the theater on Sunset and Vine to check it out. Men were working on the marquee, adding *Gary Busey* above *The Buddy Holly Story*. It took my breath away. This was the first time my name was in big lights headlining a film.

The next night, June 13, 1978, I arrived at the premiere with my wife and two best friends, Jeff Bridges and Leon Russell. Cameras flashed everywhere. The crowded lobby buzzed with people. As I took my seat in the theater, I noticed María Elena Holly, Buddy's widow, sitting at the end of the same row I was in. Being so close to her gave me a very spiritual feeling. She was the love of Buddy's life, and

Buddy was the love of her life. Now she was going to watch me relive special moments of their lives together. I was more concerned about her reaction than that of any movie critic who may have been in the audience that night. There was a little trepidation on my part because although I knew a lot of the real stories from my time spent with J. I. Allison, the movie had taken some dramatic liberties (as most movies do). I realized after getting to know Buddy's family that they supported Buddy in his music, but the movie made it seem like they didn't. It was rumored that the writer, Robert "Bobby" Gittler, had severe manic depression, so if anyone wanted to change a scene, we were told we couldn't . . . because Bobby might kill himself. Everything was done as written. Robert did eventually kill himself on May 16, 1978, right before the Dallas premiere of the movie, by a self-inflicted gunshot.

At the Hollywood premiere, as the movie played, I looked around the dark theater. It felt holy to me. Then toward the end of the movie when I sang "True Love Ways"—a song written by Buddy for his wife, María—María bolted out of the theater crying. I thought, *Oh, I messed up*. The rest of the audience, however, seemed to be mesmerized. At the end, after I sang, "Not Fade Away," I said, "We'll see you next year," then the screen freezes on my face with the words *Buddy Holly died later that night along with J. P. "The Big Bopper" Richardson and Ritchie Valens in a crash of a private airplane just outside of Clear Lake.*

In the audience, the applause was so grand it was as if a pin had burst an enormous balloon and its explosion was filled with love and acceptance.

Later in the lobby, I found María Elena Holly. She

West Coast Premiere

N° 0175

THE BUDDY HOLLY STORY

Tuesday, June 13, 1978 - 8:30 P.M.

CINERAMA DOME THEATRE
(Sunset and Vine Street, Hollywood)

ADMIT ONE

My ticket to get into *The Buddy Holly Story* premiere.

grabbed me and said, "Come here; I want to talk to you." She took me out the side doors where the trash Dumpsters were, and then with tears rolling down her face, she said, "You brought my Buddy back. You are my Buddy." I held her in my arms as she trembled and cried. In that instant, our hearts came into each other's—I am sure it was Buddy's spirit back again for the final time, right there, behind the theater next to two trash Dumpsters.

The next day, Leon Russell called me and said, "Last night I saw a star get born." He was right; not only was my performance well received by Buddy's family and widow, it was well received by the industry. I was catapulted into instant stardom. The phone rang and rang with request after request for interviews. I made the cover of *Rolling Stone*. Movie offers started rolling in, and I was invited to play music with an elite group of musicians.

One morning at 5:00, I was on my way home from playing music, driving down Pacific Coast Highway just past Heathercliff Road, when I heard on the radio the Academy Award nominations being announced.

"For the Best Actor category: Warren Beatty in *Heaven Can Wait*, Gary Busey in *The Buddy Holly Story*, Robert De

Niro in *The Deer Hunter,* Laurence Olivier in *The Boys from Brazil,* and Jon Voight in *Coming Home."* When they said my name, I was not surprised, scared, or overjoyed. I felt an enormous feeling that I am unable to put into words. Then other award nominations for Best Actor followed: Golden

With María Elena Holly at the Buddy Holly Hollywood
Walk of Fame Induction Ceremony, September 8, 2011.
(Courtesy of Seffanie Sampson)

Globes, BAFTA, Los Angeles Film Critics Association, National Society of Film Critics, and New York Film Critics Circle.

The Academy Award for Best Actor went to Jon Voight. Even though I lost, I felt like a winner because once you've been nominated, you've already won. You belong in a minuscule and elite group of awesome actors. I was up against some of the most talented men to ever grace the silver screen.

The night of the Academy Awards, Jon Voight gave me a special compliment that still lives in my heart. He said, "You know, Gary, if all four of us had to play your role of Buddy Holly, we couldn't come close."

His words made me feel like a winner. But the real award I got was the gift of playing Buddy.

21. GUITAR

Gaining Understanding
In Tunes And Rhythm

ON MY FIRST MOVIE IN 1973, shot in South Dakota, an actress had a guitar on the set. The location was at the Pine Ridge Indian Reservation. During our downtime, I borrowed her guitar and taught myself how to play. First, I learned the chords E, A, and D, then I learned G, and C, then I learned B, F-sharp and F minor. I'd been a drummer for almost a decade, so the guitar was a fresh new way to express myself. I started putting chords together, singing little songs. It was fun playing at night under the stars and the moon on that prairie. The sounds of the guitar had the ability to comfort my heart. I had no idea playing guitar would come in so handy for me five years later while doing *The Buddy Holly Story*.

The popularity of *The Buddy Holly Story* led to an abundance of great musical opportunities. I was given an all-access pass to play guitar with the most incredible musicians. Shortly after the movie, I went to see Willie Nelson play with my musician friend Stephen Bruton in Austin, Texas. Hearing Willie's music live embraced me from far, far away and put me right into Willie's heart. I was excited to meet him. Stephen and I stood in the wings watching Willie. Between songs, Willie approached us. Stephen introduced me.

"Would you like to do a song?" Willie offered.

"Sure." I went onstage with Willie and played "Rave On" with so much energy like I was still representing Buddy Holly. After the show, we went with Willie and his gang to his tour bus and burned a few down. My humor brought a unique element to his eclectic gang; I fit in perfectly. Willie and I became fast friends. The thing that struck me the most about getting to know Willie was his kind soul. He was so giving, with a great desire to make people happy. He would stand outside for an hour in the rain to sign autographs, making sure no fan got missed. Our friendship led to a movie we did together called *Barbarosa*. We always say we had a lot of fun doing it (more fun than you're supposed to working on a movie).

Post–*Buddy Holly*, I also spent a lot of time with Joel Fine, who worked on the sound for the movie. He brought me to a Bruce Springsteen concert at the Forum in Los Angeles. We arrived after the show began. As we took our seats on the side, close to the stage, Bruce was telling the audience about a movie he recently saw—*The Buddy Holly Story*—specifically the part where Buddy's mother told him he needed something to fall back on. Then, with fervor, Bruce quoted Buddy's retort to his mother—"I don't plan to fall back"—then went right into a song. Bruce was astounding. The show was astounding. I had to meet him. Backstage, we had a brief encounter where I invited him to watch me play the next day at the Sundance Saloon.

The Sundance Saloon, formerly a general store constructed in the mid-1800s, was an old rustic bar with a makeshift stage where local musicians and top entertainers stopped by unannounced to jam together. It was a potpourri of talent who loved everyone else's talent. Before *Buddy Holly*, I went there every weekend throughout the 1970s to hear music and jump onstage. I jammed with Rocky Burnette, Billy Burnette, Buzz Clifford, Kris Kristofferson, and Gene Clark from the Byrds, among many other talented musicians. When Bruce showed up. I greeted him and said, "You inspired me with the way you played last night; now I'm gonna play for you." I played three songs for him, then Bruce got up on the tiny stage to join me. To make room for Bruce, I hopped up on a bench, then Bruce hopped on a table, and we jammed together.

Whoa! There are no words to describe how incredible it was to play music with the Boss.

At this time, *The Buddy Holly Story* was still alive and well in theaters, so I was sent to Philadelphia to meet with the producers to discuss press opportunities. While I was in Philadelphia, I discovered Bruce Springsteen and the E Street Band had shows coming up at the Spectrum Arena that same weekend on August 18–19, 1978. I called Bruce to let him know I was in town. He invited me to play with them at the shows. The Spectrum was a huge venue hosting just under twenty thousand people; this would be the first time I was up front and center playing guitar and singing in such a large venue. With Leon Russell, I was always behind the drum set and never on vocals alone. It was a very big deal for me. When I joined Bruce and the E Street Band on the first night of the show, I did the song "Rave On" like a crazy acid-induced ferret on a heat-seeking missile. I was all over the place. Later that night, Bruce called and said, "Listen, I don't think we're gonna do this again tomorrow night."

"Why not?"

"It was too erratic; we really lost our place with you."

Devastated, I pleaded, "Let me do it again; you can direct me. I'll do it exactly the way you want."

He agreed. The next night, I stayed at the mic the whole time, following Bruce's direction to a T. I gained a lot of understanding from Bruce about the value of simplicity.

The flurry of opportunities, friendships, and surprises continued to roll in. Out of the blue, I got a phone call from a musical hero and neighbor of mine, Rick Danko—former bass player for the Band. The Band had a movie in the theaters concurrently with *The Buddy Holly Story* called *The Last Waltz,* directed by Martin Scorsese, documenting the Band's final concert before their ultimate breakup. My favorite groups in the world were and still are the Beatles, the Beach Boys, and the Band. It was the Band's authentic rustic, rural way of storytelling in their songs that appealed to me so deeply.

On the phone, Rick introduced himself, then said, "I want to do a tour with you, me, and Paul Butterfield."

Paul Butterfield was a historic number-one blues harmonica player from Chicago who was another hero of mine. I was a bit flabbergasted by this proposal. "Uh . . . what are we gonna do?" I asked.

"We're gonna play music."

The offer felt good to my artistic heart, so I agreed.

Although everything was unplanned, it all happened really fast. The three of us formed an instant brotherhood. I just followed their lead. Paul Butterfield, a little ball of frenetic energy, put a sensational ten-piece band together, and we started rehearsing right away at Studio Instrument Rentals in the valley. We did eight shows around town—three in

Redondo Beach and Santa Cruz, then five shows at the little hot spot on Sunset Boulevard in Hollywood called the Roxy. Our repertoire was a variation of blues songs, "Stay All Night" by B°b Wills, songs from the Band, and songs from Buddy Holly. We played with monumental energy to packed houses, two shows a night—each two and a half hours long—five nights in a row. It was like being shot out of a cannon.

My association with Buddy Holly garnered me friendships, acquaintanceships, and/or invitations to play with musical icons like Tom Petty, Bonnie Raitt, Buddy Guy, Steve Winwood, Harry Dean Stanton, Ringo Starr, Keith Richards, Jerry Lee Lewis, Paul McCartney, and more. I was hanging out, working, and creating with my heroes, truly understanding the power of rock and roll.

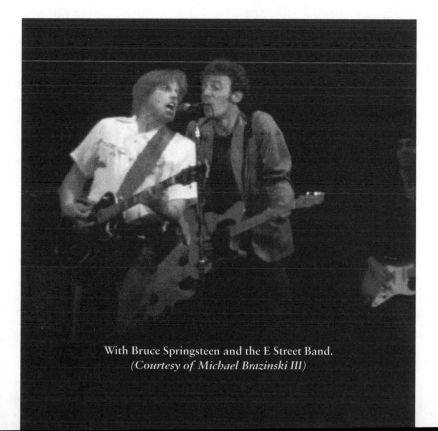

With Bruce Springsteen and the E Street Band.
(*Courtesy of Michael Brazinski III*)

With Clarence Clemons and the E Street Band.
(Courtesy of Michael Brazinski III)

Barbarosa, with Willie Nelson.

With Mom and Sir Paul
McCartney.

22. BAD

Bologna And Dirt

THE HYPE I RECEIVED FROM *The Buddy Holly Story* left me in a position to buy a nice home in Malibu, California. Judy and I chose a private community known as Malibu West located in a canyon, close to the beach. The streets were flat, and kids could play out in the open as in a forgotten era. I was home alone watching television, taking a break from all the energy swirling around me from the industry, when someone knocked at the door. I opened it to find a man I vaguely recognized wearing a cowboy hat that you'd buy in Beverly Hills, with a big sunset band around the brow. This Beverly Hills cowboy was decked out in a coat with metal emblems on the corner of each collar and a very decorated belt buckle as big as a Volkswagen hubcap.

"Hey, Gary, I'm Bob. Remember I met you at the *Big Wednesday* party?" I couldn't place him. "Remember, they call me 'the Devil.'"

"Oh, yeah." The nickname jogged my memory; he was the strange guy who followed my every move at the *Big Wednesday* wrap party. I remembered his bullshit story that he was the captain of a big boat smuggling white powder from South America, using *the Devil* as his code name.

"I've come to tell you that I'm going to be your manager."

"What?" I stared at him, mystified.

"I've got something to show you. Can I come in?"

Sadly, I said yes.

The Devil removed a Tiffany jewelry box from his pocket and presented it to me in a gracious manner, the same way Vanna White would present a new car on *Wheel of Fortune*. "This is for you." The Devil opened the box that would normally contain a big fancy ring, but it instead held an enormous chunk of cocaine, as big as an olive, with my initials, *GB,* engraved in the middle.

"I can't accept this."

"You are going to do great things in your career; this will help you."

I could probably count on both of my hands the number of times I had done cocaine at that point. The first time I ever did it was in the late '60s while in the studio recording with my band Carp. We were working with a very talented producer when he pulled me aside. "Gary, come here." He opened a little can with powder in it that looked like flour.

"What is that?"

"Cocaine."

"What do you do with it?" The hardest drug I'd ever taken was Coca-Cola.

"You snort it in your nose."

"My nose?" I was totally repulsed.

"Yes."

"Why would I do that?"

"You look tired; this will give you energy."

"I'm not putting that shit in my nose."

"Just try it; it'll make you more creative."

Any artist knows the idea of being *more* creative is too hard to refuse. I picked up the little spoon he dangled in front of me and snorted away. It burned like hell. My nose ran for hours. It was not fun and depleted my energy. I didn't get creative—in fact, just the opposite. The cocaine made me withdrawn, shy, and nonartistic. Its effects began to frighten me, then a fleeting voice invaded my mind with repetitive ceaseless queries. "What are you doing here? What are you doing here? What are you doing here?" The incessant voice was paranoid. It intensified. *"What are you doing here? What are you doing here? What are you doing here?"* I couldn't escape it. I thought if I moved around, it might go away, but it followed me everywhere. *"What are you doing here? What are you doing here?"* I was under attack in my head. Fear set in. *What if this voice never goes away?* It took hours for me to come down. It scared me so badly I didn't do cocaine again until years later while on the road with Leon Russell's band. Those few times on the road, cocaine had no big effect on me, so I didn't do it again . . .

The Devil made his way into my house, got comfortable on my green velvet couch, then removed a razor blade from his pocket. On my glass coffee table, he sliced off a piece of the large cocaine ball, chopped it up, and neatly made two straight lines with the powder. He removed a hundred-dollar bill from his wallet, rolled it up, and held it out for me to take. Up until this moment, I had always seemed to go with the flow of life, and the flow had continually led me to great success. My intuition had helped me make some great decisions and gotten me very far. I had finally reached a great place in my career. You'd think I had all my ducks in a row, but I didn't. In reality, there was ultimate confusion about everything. People were coming at me from all directions. It was difficult for me to determine the good from the bad. Being an artist, I am very suggestible, even a little gullible by nature. The temptations presenting themselves were everywhere. "Let's go to a party. Let's chase women. Let's do drugs." My intuition somehow got lost. So, as the Devil dangled the rolled-up hundred-dollar bill in my face, I made the worst decision of my life. I took it. I decided to take a *gift* from a guy I barely knew, who basically crawled out of the woodwork looking like a Beverly Hills rodeo clown that went by the name *the Devil*. I sucked the two lines of cocaine into my nose with no restrictions. I didn't think about the consequences of my behavior.

For the first time, cocaine gave me an amazing rush in my body and mind. It was beyond incredible. I felt like I could swim the length of the Mississippi River with one bathing suit. I wanted more. I partied with the Devil for hours. When he left, he said, "Keep this," and placed the Tiffany box on my desk. That night, all I could think about was that Tiffany box sitting on my desk. I had to have more. For the first time in my life, I did cocaine by myself. I spent the whole night alone in my music room doing lines. I had been introduced to the addict inside me that I had never met before, which I think we all have lurking somewhere within. It was a hard, fast introduction, but now the addict had been unleashed and was ready to take my soul.

23. LIVE

Learning In Volcanic Energy

I N 1979, I got a call from my agent, Meyer. "*Saturday Night Live* wants you to host the show in New York."

The offer was surprising. I'd watched the show religiously every Saturday night since its inception, totally in awe of the cast and what they did every week. I said, "Hell yeah." There was no chance I was going to miss the opportunity to work with the incredibly talented Not Ready for Prime Time Players John Belushi, Dan Aykroyd, Garrett Morris, Bill Murray, Jane Curtin, Laraine Newman, and the one and only Gilda Radner.

As soon as I arrived in New York City, I met the writers, the cast, and the genius at the helm of *SNL*, Lorne Michaels. During the creative process, Lorne included me every step of the way from the skits down to the musical acts. At first, I suggested that the band Little Feat be the musical guest, but then I got the idea to reprise the show I did with Rick Danko and Paul Butterfield at the Roxy. Lorne Michaels agreed. Now I was hosting and performing music, but I had no doubt I could handle it. The week was hectic,

With Gailard Sartain, Junior, and Mike Stamper. *(Courtesy of The Oklahoma Historical Society OKPOP Collections)*

working night-shift hours, but it was so filled with such artistic freedom that it was well worth it.

The process reminded me of a sketch comedy show I did earlier in my career from 1971 to 1972 called *Mazeppa Pompazoidi's Uncanny Film Festival and Camp Meeting*. *Mazeppa* happened unexpectedly, while I was in Tulsa visiting my family between acting jobs in 1971. I ran into an old acquaintance of mine from high school, Gailard Sartain. Gailard was a plump, funny guy who, in some ways, resembled John Belushi. He could take anything and turn it into a hilarious joke, then punctuate it with one of his uproarious facial expressions that always sent me into a guffaw from the deepest part of my gut. When I ran into Gailard, he brought me to the small local television station where he was currently filming *Mazeppa* along with his cohort Jim

Millaway. For the past year, they had improvised ludicrous skits with outrageously hilarious characters every week. This show was wraparound entertainment for horror films airing on Saturday nights (called Shock Theater) in Oklahoma, Arkansas, and Kansas.

"I want to be in *Mazeppa,*" I told Gailard.

"Sure." He gave me a scenario for the skit. Before I knew it, I was in front of the camera. Realizing my character didn't have a name, I called out to Gailard, "I need a name."

"Take three: Teddy, Jack, Eddy," Gailard spat without skipping a beat.

Doing the *Mazeppa* show was so much fun that over the next two years I did it every time I went to Tulsa even though I didn't get paid. Sometimes I flew myself there, on my own dime. The three of us fit together perfectly like an untailored suit. Gailard was the crazy guy creating all sorts of lunatic characters wearing bizarre wigs, doing weird stuff; Jim was the voice-of-reason straight guy; and I was Teddy Jack Eddy, whom I dubbed "the Man with the Talent."

Teddy Jack evolved into a know-it-all redneck hothead who taught people (for three dollars) everything they needed to know in order to get a job in Hollywood. I created "The Teddy Jack Eddy School for Slow Motion Fighting," "The Teddy Jack Eddy School for Airplane Noises," "The Teddy Jack Eddy School for Crying," and "The Teddy Jack Eddy School for Neat Falling" among others. At the end of every skit, Teddy Jack got enraged at Gailard's character, slapping him so hard he'd fall to the ground. Gailard always knew the slap was coming when my eyes started bulging as big as manhole covers. He would then turn his back to the camera and hold his right palm in front of his chest to signal

Saturday Night Live opening monologue.
(Courtesy of NBCUniversal Media, LLC © 1979)

he was ready for me to knock him down. I usually sent his wig (if he was wearing one) flying in the air. It became *Mazeppa*'s signature ending. Unfortunately, this was before videotapes, so most of the episodes were lost.

Mazeppa was like a preschool for *SNL*. During my week in New York, Belushi had taken me under his wing, helping

Saturday Night Live musical act with Rick Danko and Paul Butterfield. *(Courtesy of NBCUniversal Media, LLC © 1979)*

me build my confidence. We had become thick as thieves; if we weren't rehearsing, we were hanging out together at his incredibly neat, accomplished Manhattan apartment.

The night of showtime, Saturday, March 10, 1979, Belushi sent a production assistant to my dressing room ten minutes before the live show began. "Belushi wants to see you in his dressing room," he said. I figured Belushi wanted to give me a pep talk. With so little time before the show started, I bolted to Belushi's compact dressing room. There was nowhere comfortable to sit, so I stood over him. With power that could conquer the world, he gushed, "Gary, just go out there and get 'em. We got you covered!" In that moment, Belushi was filled with so much energy, it was bursting out of him like a volcano. Then he gave me a couple lines of cocaine. "Okay, now you're ready." He patted me on the back and sent me on my way. It was getting really late, so I ran my ass off to get to the set. I barely made it on time, with only seconds to spare. I sat on the bench and quickly got into character.

I wasn't fazed at all by my tardiness; however, once the live show began, a little panic set in that turned my motor on full force. It was like I'd jumped on a runaway train going 186,000 miles per second, heading to outer space. I wasn't in Oklahoma anymore. Skit by skit, I locked into each character; nothing else mattered. Everything was happening in warp speed. Before I knew it, it was time for me to do the ending musical number; then I was telling the audience, "We gotta go."

At the wrap party (held at John Belushi and Dan Aykroyd's dark, seedy private bar), I observed the Not Ready for Prime Time Players mingling about, in awe that they could do this every week. I had utilized every ounce of energy possible. It felt like I'd jumped off that speeding train I'd stepped onto at the beginning of the show, rolled through grenades, then landed in a ditch, wondering, *What the hell just happened? Can I do that again?*

Back at the hotel, it took my body a while to come down from the night. At around 5:00 A.M., I finally breathed a sigh of relief. I was wrung out but happy to have done it. I had no feelings left, but I knew it was a victory. The volcanic laughter from the audience told me that.

24. BULL

Bringing Up Life Lessons

WHILE I WAS STILL RIDING HIGH from *The Buddy Holly Story* and my Academy Award nomination, a lot of film offers came in, *all leading men.* I was in a new arena. I had always been more of a character actor, but now people wanted me to be the main squeeze. Everything was very different. I used to be able to go out in public and no one knew me; now I was literally being mobbed. I couldn't wrap my head around this new attention and fame, especially since my entire life, I'd struggled to get noticed by my dad, who never gave me one positive word of encouragement.

There were two offers on the table that I was considering. The first offer was for a movie called *Foolin' Around.* The script was not good, but the money was great, around $250,000, more than I had ever been offered before. Just coming off of *The Buddy Holly Story,* where I had only earned about $10,000 for the whole movie, my agent was really pushing for this big paycheck.

The second offer was for a movie called *Urban Cowboy.*

The producer, Irving Azoff, had been after me big-time, like a cat to a mouse, calling me at home more times than normal, trying to get me to play the lead role. In his chipper, supportive, upbeat voice, he promised this would be great for me. He said things such as: You'll get a big boost in your career. It's the perfect follow-up to *Buddy Holly*. You'll get another Academy Award nomination. I mean, he was after me hard, and even though I kept hedging back and forth, he didn't give up. He got me to thinking the part in *Urban Cowboy* really *was* perfect for me. After all, I am from Texas, and I did work on my uncle Buddy's farm when I was fourteen.

Uncle Buddy had just bought the farm where his son, Zach (in his twenties), lived with his French wife, Gisele, and her brother Jean Jacques. Zach had a 1950 convertible Chevy that I always admired. One day when my cousin Earl and I were visiting Zach, he said, "You and Earl can drive the car to the garage." He gave us very specific instructions. "Gary, you're gonna take it halfway, stop the car, put it in park, turn it off, and switch seats with Earl, who will drive it the rest of the way to the garage." The garage was only about sixty yards away, but man, this was a big-time honor for a fourteen-year-old. *I* got to drive Zach's Chevy!

Behind the wheel, I felt so grown-up; I imagined it was *my* car that I was driving into *my* garage. At the halfway mark, I kept going.

"Hey, you're supposed to stop." Earl squirmed in his seat. I just couldn't bring myself to stop; I was having ridiculous fun, but I was also driving too fast. When I turned left, I didn't see a fence made of thin barbed wire, which caused me to crash into a tree. Not only did I dent the left front fender, but a tree branch came through the windshield, hit me in head, and tore part of the convertible top. It was a disaster. I felt horrible, and so did my dad. That night at the dinner table, Dad announced, "Gary, since you did this to the car, you're going to spend the summer working with Uncle Buddy's crew hauling hay, building the barn, and herding the cattle."

I moved into Uncle Buddy's new, bug-ridden farmhouse (riddled with enormous cockroaches that marched in formation up the walls), and lived with Zach, Gisele, and Jean Jacques. I worked in the hayfields, I herded cattle, I rode on the back of a quarter horse named Easter, herding up Brahma bulls, Brahma cows, and Charolais cattle. It was a great time for me out there doing the hard work.

One day when Jean Jacques and I were taking a break from baling hay, I noticed Elvis, a beautiful teenage pure-white Brahma bull with a thick muscular neck and long curved horns, leaning against the fence in his corral. Suddenly, I got a wild hair up my ass. "I'm gonna ride Elvis." I don't know why I got the urge to ride him. I hadn't really thought about it before, but in that moment, I just wanted to see if I could do it. I'd been to so many rodeos, and it looked simple enough.

"Gary, no!" Jean Jacques was a very feisty French teenager, a couple of years older than I was, with red hair, porcelain skin, and a hot temper. He knew very little English, and I didn't know any French, but we still understood each other. He tried to stop me, but I pulled away.

"I'll be fine." I climbed on the fence next to the bull and slipped on his bare back. Since there was no saddle or reins, I held on to his ears, which I think made him furious. Instantly, Elvis took off bucking. Everything in the bull was working against me. Every movement of the bull was precise and powerful. His commitment to getting rid of me was the paradigm of all commitment. I immediately felt discomfort in my back, legs, arms, shoulders, spine, and crotch. I felt like a whip that the bull was playing with. Then suddenly, the bull stopped, did a 360-turn, started bucking again, and I was gone, shot in the air like a cannonball. This all happened in a matter of seconds. I was flung fifteen feet in the air and hit the ground hard. My right shoulder felt as though nails had been driven into it. I got up slowly so the bull wouldn't see me and made my way to the fence where there was a lariat. From fifteen feet away, I roped the bull and tried pulling him back toward me, but he was not having it. At once, he took off so fast he jerked me off the ground and dragged me around the corral like a rag doll.

"*Let go!*" Jean Jacques shouted.

I don't know why, but I hadn't thought about letting go. I released my grip on the rope, came to a stop, got up, dusted myself off, and checked my body for blood. Jean Jacques stared at me, shaking his head and screaming in French, probably, "You stupid fucking idiot!" or something to that effect.

Once I caught my breath, I said, "I'm done with the bull; let's get back to work."

After surviving a real bull, how hard could it be to ride a mechanical bull? *Urban Cowboy* was the one. I called my agent. "I can't do *Foolin' Around;* I want to do *Urban Cowboy.*"

"They're offering you a lot of money, so you're going to do *Foolin' Around.*"

"I've just done *Gumball Rally, A Star Is Born, Straight Time, Big Wednesday, Buddy Holly.* This movie doesn't measure up to any of them. I want to do *Urban Cowboy.*"

With David Busey.

There was a long beat where no one spoke, then my agent said, "Trust me; do *Foolin' Around*." My biggest fear was making a mistake in my career. So far, I had always done what my agent had told me, and we hadn't made a mistake yet. He represented the best character actors in town, plus he was a nice sharp negotiator. I trusted him. I agreed to pass on *Urban Cowboy* and signed on to do *Foolin' Around*.

When I told Irving I was committed to another movie, he was very amicable and wished me good luck. When I hung

Working for Uncle Buddy.

up the phone, my heart sank, like the feeling you get when a woman you love walks out on you.

The moment I arrived on the set, I just didn't want to be there. We shot the script as written, but nothing worked for me in the way I created characters in a movie. I was just playing myself with different clothes. I don't remember many specifics of the shoot, except one scene where they were supposed to shoot me in the crotch with a tennis ball cannon but kept missing. They must have tried thirty times until finally they hit my crotch in the right spot, where it was protected by a cup. I ended up with bruises all over my thighs and stomach. For the first time in my career, my heart wasn't in it. Each night when I got off work, I went to my hotel room and did cocaine. It was like an escape mechanism to take me out of the drudgery of this film. Finally, after a few torturous months, I finished the movie.

As I suspected, *Foolin' Around* was not exactly a box office sensation. For me, it was the worst follow-up I could possibly have done after my beloved *Buddy Holly Story*.

Urban Cowboy, on the other hand, was a smash hit. It was a piece of gold that I was too afraid to grab. I let other people influence me instead of listening to myself in that pivotal moment of my life. It was a hard lesson to swallow that hurt for a long time. Like my one and only bull ride, it bucked me, threw me, and shook me up, but once everything was all said and done, I just had to let go of the bull, get back up, check for blood, and go to work on the next film. And that's what I did.

Jake Busey with Chili Dog.

25. DOG

Dumps On Ground

I T HAD BEEN OVER THREE YEARS since the Devil had come to my house with that ball of cocaine. Since then, I had become a full-fledged coke addict. On this particular day, sometime in the '80s, Jake was at school and I had no idea where Judy was (which was good). I was free to plan my day around cocaine. I spent the morning at my desk flipping through my Filofax, reviewing the cocaine dealers I planned to visit, either to make a purchase or to take a sample. I made some calls, and my day was set. First, I would start by hanging out with some surf buddies, then I would make the trip to a dealer on Franklin Avenue in Hollywood, followed by a visit to a dealer close to home. Later, my buddy was going to come over to play music. This was my typical day if I wasn't working.

As planned, I made my rounds hanging with surfers, drug dealers, and junkies, laughing and having a ball. It had been a great day. I had three folded paper bindles in my coat pocket filled with three grams of cocaine, and music on the horizon. All was well in my world. By the time I got home, it was late afternoon. No one was there except Chili the dog, who greeted me with immense joy, jumping up and down, licking my face, pounding her large paws on my chest while making happy dog squeals.

Chili had adopted us a few years earlier when Jake was about nine. She just showed up at our door and bolted inside the house, wagging her tail, breathing heavily with her tongue hanging out of her mouth drooling saliva, smiling at us. She was a very happy dog, like a cartoon dog that had nothing but love and happiness in her. Once she bolted inside, she checked out the joint, smelling every corner, then found a spot on the couch, planted herself on it, and never left. She instantly became a member of the family, and we felt honored to have such a sweet dog adopt us. I developed a particularly close relationship with Chili, who happened to be a musically talented dog, just like me. Something about the sound of my playing really got her excited, especially the harmonica. Chili sang with me every time—in perfect key, I might add. She was a medium-sized dog, some type of a shepherd-Lab-Doberman mix, we're not really sure, with a really strange hair color that reminded me of the best bowl of chili you could get in Texas. That's how she got her name.

That day, as Chili gave me the biggest welcome home possible, somehow she stuck her paw in my jacket and pulled it off, spinning me around, then disappeared into the other room. I tried to get my footing, but I couldn't and fell flat on my belly, hitting the cold, hard tile. It left me shaken. As I collected myself, I noticed my three bindles of cocaine had been knocked out of my pocket and dumped on the ground, just out of my reach. *That's okay*, I thought, *I'll just sweep it up. I can still snort it.* That's when Chili sped around the corner.

"No, Chili, go away!" I shrieked, but Chili was moving fast, and she raced over to me, stepping through my precious powder. *"No!"* She licked me again, then ran off in a big white cloudy puff. I attempted to sweep up the remaining cocaine, but Chili rounded the corner again full force toward me.

"Get out of here!" I shouted.

Chili tackled me again and lay beside me on the floor rolling in the powder, doing a dog dance with legs kicking and flailing in the air.

"Shit!" Without thinking, I immediately swooped in like a crop duster with my nose flying first. I rolled Chili over, put my nose as deep as possible in the side of the dog, and with the strength of an industrial floor cleaner, I sucked as hard as I could. I snorted as much cocaine as I could off the dog. I sucked her back, her butt, her side—not a spot was left. I didn't get much cocaine; mostly I sucked up bugs, sticks, little bitty rocks, mud, hair, dog sweat, goo from the floor, and random unidentifiable dog debris. When I finished snorting my dog's fur, I brushed her coat and tried to convince myself that my behavior was normal. My thinking was so warped at this point that I came to the conclusion that I was brilliant for snorting my dog and saving the cocaine from being wasted. Once I composed myself, I went into my music room, played music, and snorted what little cocaine I was able to scoop off the floor, plus other miscellaneous debris. My day had been a total success.

Carny.

26. RELATIONSHIP

Really Exciting Love Affair Turns
Into Overwhelming Nightmare
Sobriety Hangs In Peril

B Y 1985, cocaine had been my main squeeze for six years. All other relationships, including with my wife and child, ran a distant second.

In the beginning, it was a very social thing to do with friends—even my wife tried it a few times. It certainly didn't feel problematic in any way. Most of the Hollywood rock star crowd I hung with was doing it. We were a team, a tribe; nothing could defeat us. We were all-powerful successful artists. The drug made us highly creative, and the common perception was that it wasn't at all addictive.

Eventually, I stopped sharing it with my friends because I wanted every last bit for myself. It became a daily habit. I'd wake up, see my drug dealers, arrive home loaded with cocaine, and play music all night in my music room or spend all night out in clubs—sometimes not sleeping for five or six days in a row. I was so wired all the time I could set up a Ferris wheel by myself in ten minutes.

At some point, I'm not quite sure when, I started to believe that I couldn't play music without cocaine. That feeling quickly escalated to everything in my life. I couldn't function without cocaine. Cocaine became my hero. It made me more imaginative, better looking, more intelligent, and a better lover, or so I thought. In truth, it was the opposite. It took all my charisma away from me. My behavior became very disturbing: I talked loudly over people, never letting them finish their sentences. I was snippy, volatile, aggressive, and short-tempered, even to loved ones. Phone conversations were brief, then I hung up abruptly. Cocaine turned me into a selfish maggot with no conscience and no feelings for others. I was pretty much an asshole even when I was sleeping. People found it difficult to be around me. I had this constant *aaarrgghhhh* feeling inside me trying to get out, chasing that first high, but I could never catch it.

Judy had no idea how addicted I'd become; her attitude at first was, "He'll finish it when he's ready." But I was never ready, and slowly my cocaine addiction tore the family apart. I'd spend weeks away from the family at clubs, sleeping in my van, crashing with friends. I pushed Judy so far away from me, every other week she kicked me out of the house. Then I'd beg and plead to come back with my cocaine ramblings, which always began with, "No, you're not listening, you're not listening, you're not listening," followed by some verbose excuse for being a terrible husband, along with promises to change that I knew I couldn't keep. She always gave in.

What Judy didn't understand was that I had become an addict, and like all addicts, I was willing to lie, steal, cheat, beg, borrow, do or say anything, to keep my addiction going. She was a kind midwestern gal from Kansas with great ideals: "Stick by my man . . . for better or for worse . . . help him get better . . . work through this, and we'll get back to those sunny days in California that we once knew." But those days never came back, and soon my wife was just plain over it. She detached from me. It got to the point where she ended up looking like the fifth face on Mount Rushmore whenever she saw me; she had nothing to say to me anymore.

I spent a lot of money on drugs. I didn't care that I was depleting the family bank accounts. When I ran out of money, I'd do another movie. It got to the point that I only worked to make money to buy cocaine. Judy and Jake suffered deeply with this addiction of mine; so did my career. The cocaine addiction made me miserable, belligerent, stupid, inconsiderate, and *so* hard to work with. I got complaints on set that I was difficult and paranoid. My reputation started to suffer. My manager would swear I was okay to work (even though I wasn't) just to keep me employed. He got calls every day from producers who said they loved my performance but were having a hard time dealing with my insanity. I knew I had a problem, but I acted like I didn't. I was convincing myself that the addiction was good. It was like being in prison without bars. By 1985, most producers weren't willing to put up with my insanity anymore, and my career hit a new low. I got cast only in low-budget movies.

I became so disconnected from myself, my desires, my goals, my wishes, my dreams, and my family, I felt like I was homeless living under a bridge next to a dead river. I missed the person I had been before being introduced to cocaine. I missed my wonderful, healthy lifestyle, always voraciously working out, jogging in the mornings, actively pursuing my career, reading *The Hollywood Reporter* and *Variety* every day, having meetings, knowing everything that was going on in the business, attending industry parties and events. I missed having every script in town on my desk.

One day in 1985, as I was leaving my house in Malibu West, with the cocaine addiction swirling heavily around me, I realized I was dying. My relationship with cocaine was killing me, and I just couldn't do it anymore. I pounded my steering wheel with an anger so deep inside of me and cried aloud, "Dear God, take this cocaine addiction away from me. Take the dealers away from me, eliminate the desire, eliminate the coke parties, eliminate everything about cocaine in my life. Take it out of my mind. I need your help. I can't do this alone."

After the angry prayer, I went on with my duties that day, visiting my manager, my agent—all without any desire to do cocaine. It was as if my angry prayer had been miraculously answered the instant I'd said it. The desire for cocaine was completely wiped out. All the muck, scabs, dirt, and mucus of the addiction were cleared away like wiping a windshield clean, leaving me shiny and brand new. I stopped calling my dealers, I stopped going to coke parties—there was no desire at all.

Unfortunately, I filled my old cocaine habit with overeating, causing my weight to balloon sixty pounds. However, newly sober, even with the extra weight, I was fun to be around again. My rapport with people got better. I listened more and talked less. Once sober, it didn't take long for me to snag a great role in Stephen King's *Silver Bullet*. My career was on the mend, and so was the most important relationship in my life—*myself*.

Lethal Weapon, 1987, with Mel Gibson and Rorian Gracie. *(Licensed by Warner Bros. Entertainment, Inc. All Rights Reserved.)*

27. MOTIVATION

Moving **O**ur **T**houghts **I**nto **V**ictory
And **T**ruth **I**n **O**vercoming **N**egativity

B Y 1986, I was enjoying one year of sobriety. Rediscov-
ering myself was like uncovering a rainbow hidden
behind a stormy sky. As the cloudy mental haze lifted, I was
able to handle my daily affairs with clean, clear, wide-open
eyes. Before sobriety, anything and everything was just an
interruption from cocaine, even work and family. The business meetings I had were fast and furious; I was only in
them to get out of them. With my new sobriety came a motivation I hadn't felt since twenty years earlier when I'd left
Oklahoma with my rock-and-roll band. I got myself back
in shape, shedding the sixty pounds I had gained. I was determined to get my career back to where it was before drugs
ravaged it.

At a birthday party for a wonderful stunt man friend I
knew from *Big Wednesday,* David Ellis, God rest his soul, I
ran into a stunt coordinator, Bobby Bass, who told me he
was stunt gaffing a new movie called *Lethal Weapon.* When
he said those two words, it triggered a feeling way deep inside of me, a little *ping* in my heart. I don't know why, but I

instinctively got the feeling that I was going to be a part of that movie. There was something about the two words *Lethal* and *Weapon* that spoke so deeply to my heart. For some reason, I really identified with those words. Deep down, I thought I was a lethal weapon. I didn't know anything about the movie; I hadn't read the script, but I had a feeling I was gonna do it. I knew there was a part for me even though I didn't know what part yet.

The next day, I called my agent, Meyer, to arrange a meeting for *Lethal Weapon*. He didn't waste ªny time getting back to me. "They agreed to meet you for the part of Mr. Joshua; we're just waiting on the details."

A little later, Meyer called again with news. "They cast the part, so the meeting is off."

"I don't believe it!"

"That's just the way it is." Meyer's words reminded me of a popular song by Bruce Hornsby and the Range called "The Way It Is" about breaking boundaries and victory. The lyrics to the song were, "That's just the way it is . . . Ah, but don't you believe them." I didn't. I couldn't believe the role that made my heart react with such a fluster could possibly be taken by another actor.

"They promised me a meeting; I want my meeting," I demanded.

"I'll call Jacob and see what I can do."

Jacob Blume was my attorney. In all the years I worked with Meyer, this was the first time he'd involved my attorney at the interview stage. I wasn't sure why, but I welcomed the extra input.

After waiting a week, I figured *Lethal Weapon* was gone, so I mourned the loss for about a minute, knowing something else would come along, as it always did. Then I got a call from Jacob Blume. "I got you the meeting for *Lethal Weapon,* but Joel Silver wants you to read a scene for them."

"Audition?" I hadn't been asked to audition for ten years, since my Academy Award nomination for *The Buddy Holly Story.* However, I wasn't going to miss this opportunity because of my ego. I was a master at cold reading. I had a great technique I learned from my mentor Jimmy Best, and I was lucky to get the meeting. "Fine, get me the script." I knew they were testing me, that I would have to knock it so far out of the park no one would know what hit them. I was more motivated than ever.

Production didn't send me the whole script, just a five-page scene where I am torturing Mel Gibson with electric shock while interrogating him about a shipment of heroin. The scene was long. The material was intense, rich, and full. I sat at my coffee table every night for a week dissecting those five pages, creating visions in my mind. I had to get this reading perfect. They were looking for someone large and menacing enough to believably go up against Mel Gibson. Although I had never actually met Mel before, I knew his work well. I'd seen him at the premiere of his movie *The Year of Living Dangerously.* Mel's energy was so strong I could feel it from afar. He was a massive acting warrior; Mr. Joshua would have to be the ultimate nemesis to even be on the same level as Mel.

When reading for a part, it is vital that the words come out of you so truthfully they are your words. Acting is the absence of acting. It is believing in the circumstances you are creating in the moment. I knew I couldn't *play* bad; bad people don't think they're bad. Instead, I considered Mr. Joshua as "misunderstood by the public." Then I created a backstory, something I always do before the movie begins, to get an idea of who the character is. It helps so I can wrap the character around me, allowing my heart to come out in the performance, leaving no acting required. Mr. Joshua's backstory was that he could walk through his grandmother's blood to get a postage stamp and never look at her. He was ice cold.

I went to Warner Bros. to read the scene for Dick Donner, the director; Joel Silver, the producer; and Marion Dougherty, the casting director. Once in the room, I said my hellos to everyone, then turned my focus on Mel Gibson, who was reading with me. I sat across from Mel, eyeing him with Mr. Joshua's shark eyes, and did the scene real quiet and evil. When we finished, they told me, "It was so cold and real, our hair stood up on the back of our necks." Then Mel grabbed me by the chest and said with a look of acceptance, "We'll see you later." Mel's reaction told me the part was mine, and sure enough, it was. I assume they paid off the other Mr. Joshua, whose identity I know not, and awarded me the glorious part.

When I finally had the complete script in hand, it hooked me instantly. I couldn't put it down. The story it told was different from most buddy cop tales. It was exciting and raw, with characters so vivid and full, I couldn't wait to get going.

Just like *The Buddy Holly Story,* this movie seemed to be guided by angels. Everything seemed to fall perfectly into place. I felt an incredible chemistry with the cast and crew. It was like being part of a symphony from heaven. Dick Donner's vision and specific attention to the minutest detail enhanced every aspect of my character. When production first dyed my hair jet black for the role, Dick said in his deep commanding voice, "I don't think the black is going to work." Dick immediately hired a top Beverly Hills hair-dresser, Jan Van Liew, also known as Jan-Girl (who still does my hair to this day), to fix it. We came up with Mr. Joshua's platinum-blond hair, which at first sight was approved by Dick. Dick never missed a trick. During the filming of my very first scene, my boss (played by Mitchell Ryan) burns my arm with a lighter. I was standing on my mark, rocking back and forth waiting for the shot to be ready, when Dick asked, "Gary, what are you doing?"

"I'm relaxing like an elephant."

"How are you relaxing? You're moving."

"When I was a teenager, I saw an elephant rocking back and forth just before the circus began; it looked like he was trying to relax."

"I want you to rock back and forth in the scene."

"Why?"

"You look like a viper." I did as Dick directed, and it was perfect. It gave Mr. Joshua a very strong, unpredictable look in his posture, as if ready to pounce at any moment.

I soon found Mr. Joshua's antagonistic character to be one of the most pleasurable roles of my career. However, I had to change a ritual of mine. Usually after a workday was over, I'd hang up the wardrobe, say good-bye to the clothes, and take the character with me everywhere I went. I always lived in my characters, which was not easy for my wife (she never knew with whom she was living). Sometimes when I'd start the day, my wife would ask, "Who are you going to be today?" But on this film, I couldn't stay in Mr. Joshua's menacing character while at home, so the ritual had to change. When I hung up the wardrobe, I made Mr. Joshua stay in the clothes. I told him, "Mr. Joshua, this is Gary going home. I will see you tomorrow." It was very harmonistic

Lethal Weapon, 1987, with Danny Glover. (Licensed by Warner Bros. Entertainment, Inc. All Rights Reserved.)

for my heart because if I carried that *misunderstood* guy within me, feeling him and believing his circumstances as I usually did, I would have made myself miserable, along with everyone else around me.

The months of filming were filled with intense focus, in a battlefield of spontaneity, all leading up to an incredible conclusion of combat using fists, feet, elbows, and heads. Dick boasted, "The fight scene is going to be a typhoon that will end the movie like no other." I understood what Dick wanted from the fight scene. Its purpose was to put a big red bow on the present that turned out to be *Lethal Weapon,* giving the movie a punctuation mark equivalent to fifty exclamation points. We began studying for the ending fight scene one month before it was shot, learning four types of martial arts: capoeira, brazilian jiu-jitsu, tae kwon do,

BUSEYISMS

and jailhouse rock. It was like learning choreography for a dance with 122 movements. However, this dance was a violent one, a dance of the titans, to the death, with people as weapons.

When it finally came time to shoot the fight scene, we did it five nights in a row, from 5:00 P.M. to 5:00 A.M. Mel and I went full speed, barely missing each other by a half an inch, an eye for an eye. We jabbed, hit, kicked, prodded, and head butted each other with a fire hydrant pelting water drops as big as fingers on us the whole time. I drove home from the studio each morning at dawn, and every time I got in the car, Bruce Hornsby's victory song, "The Way It Is," played on the radio. To me, this was an angelic sign confirming *total victory*.

Mr. Joshua lost the fight in the movie, but he won the fight for me in the movie industry. He punctuated my flailing career with fifty exclamation points, along with an explosive return of Gary Busey to the industry. A new door opened for me: the opportunity to play a villain.

When Mr. Joshua got wrapped from the movie, I felt so relieved and proud that I was given this experience. It was like going to school where you didn't study but when the test was given, you passed with an A++. The A++ came at the first screening of the movie. When I got shot, everybody in the theater clapped. I was even clapping. Then I said, "Wait a minute, I just got killed."

"That means you're a good bad guy," Mel said as we hugged each other.

A rush of championship feelings came to me, and I can only imagine it did for every single person in that room who worked on *Lethal Weapon*. It was one of the big jewels in the artistic crown of my achievements and one of the extreme highlights of my career—plus, it put me back on the A-list.

When they were developing the sequel, we discussed the possibility of bringing Mr. Joshua back, but unfortunately, he got shot right in the heart, dying instantly. I tried to talk Mel Gibson and Dick Donner into a twin brother who lived in Brazil with six rhesus macaque monkeys working for him, but they were laughing too hard to buy the scenario. I guess that's just the way it is.

I would also like to share a quote I heard from an interview with Dick Donner that touched my heart so deeply:

"Gary Busey is again one of those wonderful strange apparitions that comes into your life and becomes a touchable reality and you want to hang on to him forever."

Lethal Weapon, 1987. (Licensed by Warner Bros. Entertainment, Inc. All Rights Reserved.)

28. ROMANCE

Relying On Magnificent And
Necessary Compatible Energy

*L*ETHAL WEAPON BLEW MY CAREER wide open. It was
just the revival I needed. In 1988, the next movie I
signed on to do was called *Act of Piracy*. Production had
already selected Belinda Bauer, a beautiful model turned
actress, to play the female lead role, but per my contract, I
had to approve of her. I was familiar with Belinda. Not only
was she one of the top Revlon models of the day, I had also
seen her in two knockout performances (both in movies
with my buddy Jeff Bridges). Production set up a lunch
meeting at a restaurant in Santa Monica. I arrived on time,
as usual, due to my military upbringing. I scanned the room
for the raven-haired beauty, but she was not there. Five minutes passed, then ten, then fifteen, then a lot more.

By the time Belinda finally arrived, she had kept me waiting forty-five minutes. I don't know why she was late—she
did not offer that information. Instead, she flashed a beautiful smile, gave me a quick apology, shook my hand, and
said, "Hello, I'm Belinda Bauer." She was really dressed
down, as if she were trying to hide her body, but still she

was a knockout. The way Belinda's wavy chocolate-brown hair framed her porcelain skin reminded me of a princess. Her soft, tender voice sparked my imagination with visions of a magical entity flying around spreading pixie dust. Her overall demeanor was vulnerable and withdrawn. I could tell she didn't want to come off too strong to get the part. It didn't matter how she came off; I already knew I wanted her for the part.

Our meeting flew by. For the next two hours, our conversation flowed like a lazy river. With a sparkle in her hazel eyes, she told me about her accomplishments as a young dancer in school. I could see she felt good about herself, talking about the projects she had done in the past. The more she told me, the more I became impressed, and the more I wanted to know about her. Since the course of natural conversation came so easily I knew acting together would be a snap. I said, "I want you for the part."

"Oh!" An uninhibited smile flooded her face, and her body loosened. Without any words, I could see the excitement take over Belinda's body. In an instant, she went from shy and withdrawn to wide open. Sparks of acting promise flew between us.

"Okay, I'll tell the producer that I approve and you're gonna be in the movie."

Over the next two months, Belinda and I met several times a week to prepare for the shoot. Mostly the meetings took place at Belinda's home in Santa Monica. She lived in a modest but full guesthouse behind a larger house. With the wall of not being chosen gone, we were able to work together, on the same level, dissecting the script, running lines, getting into the emotions of our characters, and sharing ideas. Every day was creatively better than the one before; it became a passion project for us. We were in a free-range country of complete imagination for the purpose of creating an authentic, good movie. To make matters even better, we found out our location was going to be on the Greek island of Skiathos in the northwest Aegean Sea.

I couldn't wait to go.

I had been clean and sober for three years at this point, but my sobriety only accentuated a looming unhappiness in my marriage. Judy and I barely spoke anymore. With the upcoming three-month shoot in Greece, it became very important to me that I leave on good terms with Judy. Although I still secretly harbored feelings that I had been somewhat forced into the marriage in the first place, I really wanted to patch things up so we could have love in our hearts while I was away. However, Judy was just too upset with me to be receptive. When the limo arrived to take me to the airport, I tried to break through to her one last time before leaving for Greece. "Judy, I don't know what to do. Please. Talk to me, tell me what I can do." I walked around the house crying.

"I have nothing more to say to you." She spoke without emotion.

I can only guess our rift was the result of a premature marriage between two young and un-evolved people along with years of drug-induced disappointments that had taken their toll on Judy. Whatever it was that was upsetting her, I'm positive it was my fault. I couldn't break through. I left the house in tears. As I drove to the airport, a feeling came over me that I wasn't coming back here again.

I arrived in Skiathos at the end of the vacation season. The island was fairly unoccupied. The cast and crew took over an enormous luxury hotel overlooking the beautiful

Aegean Sea. My room was magnificent, with big open doors leading to a grand balcony overlooking the water. Alone in my palatial breezy room, with no one there, I could take a deep breath of the fresh sea air and let go of everything I had left behind at home. It was just the relief I needed.

I had a week before filming began, so production gave me a little Peugeot to tool around the island in. Since Belinda was the only one I knew, she accompanied me in my explorations. We raced around in the tiny car, discovering churches, visiting archaeological ruins, eating in secluded open-air waterfront Greek cafés. It was the first time we spent together not as costars but as regular people enjoying life on the island, exploring a new land together, sharing meals together, laughing together, enjoying the beauty around us. I quickly began to feel something different stirring between us.

When filming began, we went into full work mode. After long days on the set, I usually had a meal with Belinda and then went to sleep. One night after dinner, I walked Belinda to her room, fifty feet from mine. "Would you like to come inside and listen to Siddha yoga music?" Belinda offered.

"I don't know what that is."

"It's very relaxing."

I couldn't refuse. When I entered her room, the ambience was striking. She'd decorated the space with colorful silk shawls on all of the lampshades, creating an exotic atmosphere of romance. Belinda put Billie Holiday music on and then sauntered to the bed, flipping the covers back. "This is where we're going to be now. In bed." Her subtle yet assertive seduction was like nothing I had experienced with a woman before. I was married very young, before I was ready, before I had experienced anyone else. I was in a hazy dream of joy and surprise being with this angel in this erotic room overlooking an exotic land. We united physically, mentally, emotionally, and spiritually. It felt nothing but good, natural, and enlightening, like it was meant to be. From that night until the movie wrapped, Belinda and I were like two moons that created high tides, soul mates from many lifetimes, never apart. What grew in my heart for her was a complete surprise to me.

When it was time to go back home, Belinda made it known that she was not going to be the other woman. Psychologically, I was already headed in the direction of a divorce, but I wasn't quite ready to do it yet. When I returned home, Judy greeted me with home-baked chocolate chip cookies, dressed in short shorts and a tight tank top. It was obvious that whatever bad feelings Judy had for me before I left were gone on her part and that she was sincere in her attempt to try to patch things up. But I was back home with my body, not with my heart. I wanted to be there for the family but Belinda was like a magnet pulling my heart toward her. I longed to be across the bay with Belinda in her comfortable little home in Santa Monica.

This was no ordinary attraction. My connection with Belinda was so strong it went past the zone of feelings. Our energies together were like a big, beautiful, spinning golden egg, and I agreed with the feeling. I couldn't stay away from her. I spent most of my days with Belinda, knowing it would only be a matter of time before I was strong enough to make the move out of Judy's life and into Belinda's forever. At the same time, Judy couldn't live in denial anymore. She knew about the romance with Belinda. Back then, having an affair and getting away with it was more difficult; there was no texting or emailing. If I wanted to connect with Belinda, I had to call her from the house and lie about whom I was talking to. Judy knew what I was up to. After a certain point, she finally put her foot down and let me know she wasn't that stupid.

We decided to separate. I moved into a small house on Pacific Coast Highway, and for the first time in my life, I lived alone.

With Belinda Bauer.

29. GIFT

Guidance In Future Travel

A FTER *ACT OF PIRACY* WITH BELINDA, I signed on to shoot an HBO miniseries in the Philippines about the assassination of Benigno Aquino called *A Dangerous Life*. I brought Belinda with me. Unfortunately, the nature of the material was so intensely political that my life became threatened, requiring bodyguard protection every minute of the day. Midway through the shoot, the dangerous atmosphere in the Philippines forced production to relocate to Sri Lanka. When the show was completed, Belinda wanted to visit her family in Australia. After such an intense shoot, a family trip was just what I needed. My romance with Belinda was stronger than ever, and meeting her parents would really solidify everything. The trip to Australia did a great job of washing the tension from the movie away. It was a real pleasure seeing where Belinda came from and getting to know her roots.

After a very satisfying time in Australia, we headed back to the States on Qantas Airways with one brief stop in Tahiti. When the big 747 landed in Tahiti, the stewardess (yes, we called them stewardesses in the '80s) came over to me in the upstairs first-class section and said, "Mr. Busey, you have a *big* surprise coming."

"A big surprise?"

"Marlon Brando is going to be sitting across the aisle from you on the flight to Los Angeles."

The Marlon Brando?

I have only been starstruck twice in my life. The first time was in the early '70s at the beginning of my acting career, probably around 1973. I was going to Universal Studios to see a screening of a television movie I'd just completed called *The Law*. I drove up to the guard gate in my van.

"What's your name?"

"Gary Busey."

"How do you spell that?"

"*B-U-S-E-Y*." The guard was older, and he moved slowly, checking the list for a long time.

"You're not on the list; you have to be on the list to get on the lot." I was so green at the time I didn't know what to do or whom to call. Then in front of that guard stand stepped a man with such charisma and power in his posture, smile, and eyes. It was Burt Lancaster.

"Find his name—*Busey*. B-U-S-E-Y." Burt Lancaster stood over the guard checking the list. "There it is." Burt pointed to my name and then turned to me and said, "Remember that we met here. This will be the last time you'll ever need help getting onto a lot; you're going to be a big star." Burt stuck his hand out to shake mine. Sheepishly, I took his hand through the window of my van. It was warm, his grip perfect—not too soft, not too strong. "Keep on," he said. Then he left. Hearing those words come out of the mouth of Burt Lancaster, an icon since the motion picture industry began (whom I had watched *so* many times before in interviews and movies), sent me reeling into rookie shock. I didn't know if Burt actually saw my movie or not, but he definitely saw me, he saw my heart. Getting a gift from a man like that gave me a lot of self-respect.

The second encounter came one day in 1978. Billy Katt, Jan-Michael Vincent, and I were eating sushi at a place in Malibu after a day of filming *Big Wednesday* when a blond man with a thick, full beard and crazy, long, wiry hair leaned out and said, "Hey, man, I saw you in that football movie. Your eyes are strong, the way you don't blink. You have the goods, son. You have the goods."

"Thanks, man." None of us recognized the man at first until we noticed he was sitting next to Ali MacGraw.

We whispered to each other like little children, "Is that Steve McQueen? Oh my God, that is Steve McQueen!" The man stood up. "Shhh, he's coming over."

Standing right behind me, Steve gently massaged my shoulders. "I'm Steve McQueen."

"I'm Gary Busey." I was timid, almost too embarrassed to say my name because it didn't hold the same power Steve McQueen's name did. We spoke about the business for probably fifteen minutes. He told us he wanted to have a seminar to help new actors in town, to teach them about the executives, the sharks, and the lying that goes on. Steve was very cut-and-dried, then he said, "The two worst words you can hear in Hollywood are *trust me*." With that, he stopped massaging my shoulders, looked me straight in the face without blinking, and said, "I want you to know that you can do this thing; you can do it well. At this time, I'm passing my torch on to you." He sat back down at his table, collected a few things, then left with Ali by his side. Once again, I reeled in rookie shock. The King of Cool gave me the gift of his guidance, blessings—and his torch.

When the stewardess told me Marlon Brando was about to sit next to me for the next eight or so hours, my stomach shot to my throat. *The* Marlon Brando, a hero of mine, someone I actually idolized. I felt like I was in ninth grade all over again, at my very first football game, wondering how I was going to do. I was already a little intimidated.

When Marlon arrived, for a moment there was no air left to breathe, then a big gasp of excitement. He was big, rotund, with thinning hair that flowed down the sides of his head, but he had that *Brando* face. That powerhouse Brando face. Every part of Marlon's face exposed feelings in him that he wasn't trying to give. His face was like a rainbow of emotions. Entranced, I watched him get comfortable in his seat. He glanced at me with a spark of recognition. "Hey, Nick."

I have been called Nick, or Mr. Nolte, ever since my career began. Ironically, Nick Nolte is a great friend of mine. When I met him in the early '70s, it was like looking in the mirror. We were both the same size, blond, intense, rugged types of guys. Nolte and I ran together in the '70s and '80s, usually at parties, staying all night, wearing identical matching straw hats of unknown origin. Whenever a party ended, usually at two in the morning, we wouldn't leave, so Nolte and I became known as "the Things Who Wouldn't Leave." You could usually find us under the kitchen table laughing, with our straw hats on. Nobody ever had the nerve to ask us to leave, so when everyone was gone and the lights were off, we figured out it was time to go. We were like cartoon characters, sharing a common element of fun, dares, and tricks. Usually when people mistook me for Nolte and I got the "Hey, Nick," or "Mr. Nolte, you were great in *48 Hrs.*" or "How's your son, Brawley, doing?" I just smiled and told them I was Gary Busey. I even got Nolte's fan mail, and if time permitted, I sent it back signed. As of this writing, I am still recognized as Nolte on a weekly basis, and I'm sure the same goes for him. Personally, it's an honor. He is an extremely talented artist. It doesn't even bother me that people think Nolte's crazed mug shot is mine. Who cares what people think? Okay, I will admit, for the first time, with Brando sitting next to me, I cared what *he* thought.

"I'm not Nick; I'm Gary Busey. Nick and I are good friends."

"I would hate it if anybody called me a name that wasn't mine."

"I'm also in the professional acting business."

"What have you done?" Marlon seemed genuinely curious.

"*The Buddy Holly Story.* I played the guitar and sang the songs in the movie the way Buddy did, as best I could."

"You really sang?"

"Yes."

"That's beyond acting."

I was very humbled speaking with Marlon, the master. I could watch *A Streetcar Named Desire* twenty times. Marlon created an essence that made it seem like I was watching it for the first time; that's how incredibly talented he was.

Marlon opened up to me. He told me stories about his career—*Last Tango in Paris, The Godfather, Apocalypse Now.* When Marlon spoke, it was like the Buddha was speaking, not because he was three hundred pounds but because he *was* the Buddha, the Buddha of acting. I was with the greatest teacher alive, and he was giving me a profound lesson in terms of making a performance authentic and free, with no acting required. "Gary, let me tell you this: Life is a rehearsal—you're just making it up as you go. Don't let anyone steal your thunder. If your thunder gets stolen, you will have no storm to give." I wrote every word he said down because I knew I was receiving essential guidance that I needed to keep forever.

After our talk, Marlon slept the rest of the way, and I spent my time basking in the unexpected seminar I had received from the master. When we landed in Los Angeles, there were no big parting words; Marlon glanced at me with a different spark of recognition from before and simply said, "Nice flying with ya."

All three movie icons were angels sent to guide me, each at a certain time to confirm I was on the right path. What struck me most about them was their desire to use their expertise to help. Your angels appear in many different forms to give you just what you need to propel you forward in the right direction.

30. LIFE

Living In Forever Eternity

MY FIRST EXPERIENCE WITH BIKES was in the early '80s. I had a green dirt bike that I rode through the hills behind my house to hang out with Nick Nolte, who lived right across the way. In 1987, I upgraded the dirt bike for a motorcycle. A beautiful custom-painted black, cream, and red Heritage Softail, Harley-Davidson—the Cadillac of Harleys. The bike was custom made for me with a Sioux Indian arrow painted on the gas tank under the Harley-Davidson logo to signify I was a warrior, because that's how I felt riding it. I loved the freedom to go wherever I wanted, whenever I wanted, on the back of that bike with the wind blowing on me. All my questions were answered with the freedom of that bike. I was an invincible captain of victory riding a powerful machine roaring down the street. From the start, I felt very comfortable on my Harley. I trusted my quick mind, athletic ability, coordination, and reflexes to keep me safe on the road, plus I took all the necessary defensive driving courses.

I had lots of riding buddies, including Arnold Schwarzenegger and Mickey Rourke. Arnold and I tried smoking cigars while we rode, but the wind blew the burning end right into our faces, so we decided to lose the cigars. Mickey was my favorite riding buddy of all. We rode throughout the hills of Malibu, usually ending up at the Rock Store on Mulholland to get grub. We both didn't have baffles in our mufflers, making us so loud nobody would ride behind us, which we thought was great. I mostly rode for joy, but eventually even though I had a car, my preferred method of travel was the Harley.

By late 1988, my career was on a real upswing. My villainous role as Mr. Joshua in *Lethal Weapon* sparked a lot of attention along with a new concept of hiring me to play bad guys. I accepted a role in the movie *Hider in the House* to play a deranged psychotic killer opposite Mimi Rogers. I spent two months on location in Monrovia, California. After the movie wrapped, I arrived home on a Friday night, December 2, 1988, to be exact. I took all day Saturday to recover, unpack, and unwind. By Sunday, feeling really good about having the movie in the can, I was ready to get back to my life, specifically Belinda and my Harley. Before I'd left to make the movie, I'd taken my Harley to Bartels' Harley-Davidson in Culver City to install a new windscreen and have it serviced. This particular Sunday, December 4, 1988, was an unusually gorgeous, tropical day in California. After being on location for so long, it was very important to get my bike back right away. I couldn't wait until Monday. Even though I knew Bartels' was closed on Sundays, I called my buddy Gene Thomason, who worked there, at his home around 10:00 A.M. to find out if he would open the shop especially for me. Gene, a fun, humorous guy about my age with poofy red hair, had become my friend since I patronized Bartels'. He agreed to meet me there at 11:00 A.M., on his own time. I called a cab, and then I had a quick conversation with Belinda. We decided I'd go over to see her after I picked up the motorcycle. I quickly got dressed in my motorcycle uniform—Levi's, sweatshirt, boots, and my favorite beige leather jacket, built more for fashion than safety. I grabbed a pair of leather gloves and my goggles, then headed out the door into the cab.

I arrived at Bartels' right on time at 11:00 A.M. My bike was parked on the sidewalk, its glistening, shiny chrome inviting me to play. I went inside, where Gene was waiting for me. We had a nice talk, laughed as usual, then headed outside. On the way out of Bartels', I noticed a rack of helmets and thought, I *should get one of those . . . next time.* At 11:39, I sprung on my Harley and hit the starter. It sounded real good, growling like a beast on the sidewalk. Everything was in tune, tightened, ready to ride. I yelled over the loud engine, "Thanks, Gene! I feel great having my bike back!" I waved good-bye to Gene, then drove down Washington Boulevard, reaching about forty miles per hour.

At 11:40 A.M., only fifty feet away from Bartels', I crashed.

This is what I remember: When I left Bartels', I didn't want to go left across traffic on Washington Boulevard because it was busy and seemed too dangerous, so I went right instead, then made a U-turn, passing Gene waving at me in front of Bartels' heading toward Robertson Boulevard, where I planned to catch the freeway. I was told I drove around a bus (I don't remember the bus) to go right on Robertson Boulevard, when I hit some sandy gravel on the road, which caused the back of my bike to fishtail. That is when everything happened suddenly, in slow motion, like watching a football play in slow mode. As the bike fishtailed, I just wanted to stop it, so I hit the rear brake. That made the bike lean too far down to the right. I didn't want to fall to the side, so I hit the front brake, which caused me to flip over the handlebars. I hit headfirst, followed by my pelvis, on the curb—right at the feet of a policeman who happened to be there, scouting the route of an upcoming marathon race. I have no memory of anything else, even though I was still conscious.

This is what I was told happened after I crashed: The policeman called the paramedics, who happened to be only one block away, eating hamburgers on their lunch break. My buddy Gene, who saw the whole thing happen, sprinted toward me and noticed the right side of my skull was cracked open from my ear to the top of my head with a hole in the middle that was spurting blood. To try to stop the bleeding, he grabbed one of my gloves and stuffed it in the hole.

I struggled to get to my feet while repeating, "I want to get up, I want to get up," before I went unconscious. The paramedics arrived lightning fast, then took me to Cedars-Sinai, where I underwent emergency brain surgery by Dr. Lauren Hooten. The surgery, which lasted two hours, treated subdural hematomas in my brain. *Subdural hematoma* is the medical term for a massive collection of blood outside of the brain, under the skull, a.k.a. blood clots. Then, bone was removed from my pelvis to fill up the hole in my skull (I am truly a butthead). The doctor told my family if I had arrived just three minutes later, I would be dead, but he still only gave me a 2 percent chance of surviving the next forty-eight hours. He also said if by some miracle I did live, I would most probably be a vegetable or paralyzed on my left side.

During this time, I quit living and left my earthly body.

Outside of my body, my essence was eighteen inches long and a quarter of an inch wide, which is the making of your soul that lives in the column of your spine. I found myself in a room with unlimited space, filled with balls of light. I understood the balls of light to be angels. With the angels surrounding me, I felt the most relaxed I had ever been, like I was in paradise being showered with feelings of love, trust, kindness, protection, safety, and guidance. I knew I was still alive, in a very special place—"the other side . . . the spiritual realm . . . the supernatural." In the distance, lunar-colored figures, the same size as my essence, were lined up. Instinctively, I knew they were my past relations that had been with me on earth who had transitioned here before I had.

I did not see with eyes; I saw with feelings.

In a moment, I slowly became surrounded by three balls of light, one golden, one magenta and amber, one abalone and mother-of-pearl, that were floating, breathing, and radiating loving energy I had never felt before. Out of the globes of light came an androgynous voice I cannot impersonate, but will never forget, that spoke to me in *thought*.

It said, *You are in a place of recovery. For the responsibility you have to mankind, it is time for you to look for help in the spiritual realm. You may come with us now or return to your body to continue your destiny.* A heavenly gap of silence ensued, then the androgynous voice continued with great love and understanding. *It's your choice.*

My spirit listened very closely to every word the androgynous voice said. I knew I was receiving important instructions to send me forward and upward. I had to decide if I wanted to live or die. Once the angel said, "It's your choice," with such great love—*bam*—I immediately went back in my body. In the supernatural, you don't *think* about things, you feel; and you feel very, very good. The second I heard the truth, I immediately accepted it and went toward it. I knew I had a lot more to do on earth, so I made the choice to come back. I could live my life here on earth to accelerate happiness, joy, and positivity like never before. Any fear about death was erased. The most important thing I learned after my death is that *death* is just an earth word. You never really die. The soul in your earthly body moves on to a different plateau. Life is forever.

On my Harley, two months before the accident.

31. BABY

Being A Beautiful You

THE MONTH FOLLOWING THE MOTORCYCLE ACCI-
DENT, I was in a coma, so I don't remember exactly
what happened, just what I've been told by my family and
friends.

While I was having brain surgery, no one knew what was
going to happen. Even though we were still separated, my
wife came to the hospital with my son Jake to be by my
side. Quasi-celebrity journalists of the day, such as Rona
Barrett, silently lurked the waiting area, hoping for a scoop.
When the brain surgery ended, I was moved into the ICU on
life support in a coma. It had been determined that not only
were there blood clots, there was also an injury to the brain
itself, and my pelvis had been shattered. The doctors
couldn't make any promises that I would ever come out of
the coma; in fact, they told my family to prepare for the
worst. However, the question remained: If I did live, how
would this affect my personality, my talent as an actor, and,
most of all, my abilities as an able-bodied person? The

particular area of the brain that had been damaged, controlled attention, perception, memory, impulse control, social competence, and *musical ability*. Doctors told my family, "*If* he pulls out of this, his personality traits will be magnified, and he won't be as talented musically."

Immediately after the surgery, I was a scary sight. I resembled a pumpkin-head science experiment, with my cranium covered in gauze bandages, tubes sticking out draining blood amid other yellowish fluids, and wires taped to my chest. Jake recalls being in the room with me the first night and putting his hand in my hand, and in my unconscious state, I did a very faint three-step handshake that I always did with him (a regular shake followed by a sideways thumb grab, which ended with our fingers locked together like a train coupler). It was my first movement since the crash. Jake said in that moment, he knew his dad would be okay.

Over the weeks I remained in a coma, my family held vigil for me. Always by my side were Judy; Jake; my brother, David; my sister, Carol; and Mom. Belinda came to the hospital, too, but it was awkward with Judy there, so Belinda respectfully bowed out, allowing Judy the opportunity to be the wife helping her husband.

Around Christmastime, I awoke from the coma. It had been three weeks since the accident. I am unsure of the duration of my encounter in the supernatural. The entire occurrence felt three minutes long, but it could have been three hours, three days, or the whole three-week period that I was in the coma. I will never know.

I was transferred to a head trauma unit in the hospital. There was a very long road to recovery ahead of me. I lost my abilities to walk, talk, and swallow. As my brain started the healing process, I experienced extreme bouts of agitation. Unable to speak, I mumbled and grumbled unintelligible words, sometimes shrieking to communicate with people. No one understood me, which made me extremely anxious. I didn't want the nurses touching me, but most of all, I didn't want to be in the hospital. Once I started getting my movement and strength back, I tried to fight my way out of the hospital any way I could. My emotions were out of control. The doctors didn't know how to contain me, so I was moved to the psych ward, where there was a lockable door. When I got out of hand, I was stripped naked, tied to the bed with shackles, and drugged with a cocktail of psychotropic medication to sedate me—basically inducing another coma as needed to contain my agitation. I spent the next week in a wheelchair insensate, with eyes glazed over, drifting off looking like a cutaway shot from *One Flew Over the Cuckoo's Nest*.

My brother, David, didn't agree with the treatment I was receiving, being drugged and isolated in the psych ward. An orderly warned David that I was under too much medication. The family decided to sneak Dr. Edward Wagner, a pioneer in alternative holistic medicine (and my chiropractor at the time) into the psych ward to get a bead on what was really going on with my brain. Dr. Wagner, who had been treating me for years, concurred with the orderly, that I was on too much medication. Dr. Wagner felt the agitation I experienced was a natural process necessary for the brain to heal itself and that medication was actually preventing my healing process from happening. Unfortunately, the hospital refused to take me off the medication, so the consensus was to find a hospital better equipped to treat my brain injury—with lockable doors. My family drove up and down the streets of Los Angeles looking for the right hospital that could contain me in a peaceful way, which is how they came across the Daniel Freeman Memorial Hospital.

My family had me transferred to Daniel Freeman in Inglewood to be treated by Dr. Barry Ludwig and Dr. Roger Light in the brain injury unit. Daniel Freeman was like a hospital without hospital rooms. There were no hospital-type beds, and no sterile hospital vibe. Instead, the rooms were single dorm-style apartments with a bedroom, dresser, table, and bathroom.

My new doctors immediately took me off most of the medication so they could start working with me. It was a grueling period of rehabilitation. I had to start over again, like a baby, relearning all the things we do on a daily basis (and take for granted) such as eating, talking, and walking. It was the normal things (that come easily) that were the most difficult for me as I transitioned from a comatose vegetable into a functioning human being again. Just learning how to open a dresser drawer, get a shirt, and put it on was taxing.

Although I had been out of the coma for two weeks, I was still not back to full consciousness until January 8, 1989, on Elvis Presley's birthday. I remember that all of a sudden while walking across my hospital room, I just came back. Instantly, an uneasy scattered feeling consumed me. I vaguely remembered . . . something happened on the motor-cycle that wasn't good. I barely recognized my family. I knew they were important people, but that was the extent of my memory. I carried an intense trepidation that I would die at any time. One night while I was sitting on my bed, a figure appeared standing in the corner of my room. It was an apparition of the grim reaper. He was taller than I was, about six foot six, holding a large sickle over his head. He lifted his hand and pointed directly at me. I heard his voice say, in thought, *Relax; it's not your time to go.* Then his arm went down, the blade above his head began spinning, and he slowly melted away. After his visit, the uneasy, scattered trepidation of death I had been feeling left me.

At this point in my recovery, walking had become much easier, but speaking and eating were tough. I remember people feeding me, but I wanted to eat on my own. Frustrated, I started storing green beans in my upper lip to save for later so I wouldn't starve. My coordination was terrible. Learning how to hold a fork and put it in my mouth was nearly impossible. Eventually, I started using invisible utensils and ate invisible food, which satisfied me immensely.

Not under sedation, I was able to make good progress, as I was finally allowed to go through that intense period of agitation, but I was a lot to handle. I'd roam the halls or suddenly barge into other patients' rooms, pillage their drawers, or rearrange stuff. Sometimes, I'd make patients get out of bed and get dressed while they were trying to sleep. In my mind, I was being useful, helping them organize. My wife realized I needed to be busy doing something. She told Dr. Ludwig, "He's an actor; tell him he's playing a doctor in a movie, let him go on rounds with you to prepare." Dr. Ludwig agreed it could be a creative way to keep me out of trouble.

Dr. Ludwig gave me a white lab coat with a clipboard and pencil and let me follow him on his rounds. I was very diligent, my son says, almost comical to watch. Sporting my shaved head with patches of hair growing in strange places, big bandages on my skull, a hospital gown under the lab coat, barely able to talk, visiting patients, rambling my diagnoses while scribbling unintelligible gibberish on a clipboard. Nothing I said made sense to anyone, but to me it was serious medical stuff. Every day, the doctor told me, "Gary, you're doing a movie playing a doctor, and you're going to make rounds with me to prepare for the role." And every day, I went to work with Dr. Ludwig, meticulously preparing for my upcoming movie.

One day, during my rounds with Dr. Ludwig, I created my very first Buseyism for the word *neat*. While Dr. Ludwig was talking to a patient, I decided to organize the patient's sock drawer. The drawer was a disaster. I paired all the socks, then lined them up nice and neat. At the time, I was just getting my words back in a cohesive manner, and as I organized I said, "Nice . . . Exciting . . . And . . . Tight—NEAT."

Making rounds was a vital part of my recovery. For the first time since becoming conscious, I had a job to do—playing a doctor. It gave me a purpose that relaxed me, helped channel my energy, and controled my agitation. Soon I stopped roaming the halls and raiding other people's rooms.

When I wasn't making rounds, I was on a good routine of occupational therapy, speech therapy, physical therapy, and brain exercises. After a short while, I got my memory back. It was very comforting to remember my family. They taught me simple words on flash cards. I'd make crazy sounds that slowly turned into words, like a baby. Every time I turned the corner with my speaking and enunciation of words, I got great accolades from my family, like a baby.

Through hard work, excellent treatment, help, prayers, and love from family and friends, I was released from the hospital three months ahead of schedule, on February 4, 1989. It had been a mere two months since the day I'd split my skull on that curb on Washington Boulevard. Doctors said they had never seen improvement this fast on a brain injury as severe as mine in their entire careers. Dr. Ludwig felt it was a miracle. He had no idea how I recovered so quickly. Neither do I. I walked myself out of the hospital a changed man. I knew I shouldn't be here, but I was, with another chance at life—a rebirth mentally, emotionally, physically, and spiritually. I was opening a new book of life.

I am often asked how I have changed or what I do differently since the accident. First off, I always wear a helmet. I wear a helmet when I take a shower, I wear a helmet when I tie my shoes, and I wear a helmet to bed because you never know when you are going to hit your head. People say I'm funnier now, too. But truly, when you get that close to death, you earn a whole new introspection and perspective about life. Anything is possible here on earth, and miracles happen every day if you are willing to see them.

March 1, 1989, press conference opposing the mandatory helmet law. *(Courtesy of Michael Grecco / MGP, Inc. / Michael Grecco.com)*

32. LAW

Losers And Winners

M Y WIFE RENTED AN EXTREMELY LARGE HOUSE in the Malibu Country Estates after we separated. She had hopes that we could start fresh in a new home once I was finished with my midlife crisis. Upon my release from the hospital, my family took me to the new house to recover, thus ending our separation (not quite how we had planned to end it, but nonetheless that's how it happened).

Not long after I was released from the hospital, on March 1, 1989, I made my first public appearance at a news conference at the Beverly Hills Hotel *opposing* the mandatory helmet laws that were being introduced. Before the accident, I actively campaigned against helmet laws. Now, only three months after I'd split my skull on Washington Boulevard, at the urging of a few people, I publicly confirmed that I was *still* against the helmet law—a statement many other people wondered about.

I spewed a slew of nonsense at the conference: "If I was wearing a helmet, I could have been more seriously injured . . . I could have broken my neck with a helmet on . . .

I could be a vegetable right now if I wore a helmet . . . Helmets impair peripheral vision" . . . yada yada yada. I spouted garbage after garbage, and then when asked if I would continue to oppose helmet laws, I answered, "My position is still pro-choice, although I believe helmets should be mandatory for riders ages sixteen to twenty-one because they are more reckless." What crap! Who was more reckless than I was?

Everything I said was a distortion of my truth. I didn't know my position at the time. I was still in recovery, still processing the ordeal. Details of what I went through in the hospital were just starting to come back to me. I was suffering short-term memory lapse. I didn't know my position. I barely knew who I was.

In contrast to all my injuries, my Harley-Davidson was just fine after the crash. Needing very few repairs, it was back in my garage waiting for me to take it on the road. Growing up in Texas and Oklahoma, the motto was: "When you fall off a horse, get back on and ride so the fear doesn't stay with you." That's exactly what I did; I got back on my Harley and rode again—*without a helmet.* After almost losing my life, getting back on that bike was a great achievement and victory, but very scary. I rode for a short while; however, it didn't feel right to me anymore. Being on that bike without a helmet made me feel exposed, naked, reckless, and just plain stupid. Unfortunately another thing that didn't feel right to me was being back with my wife. She was instrumental in my recovery, and I appreciated her help very much, but I just couldn't do it anymore. I moved back to the tiny place I had lived in before the accident, on Pacific Coast Highway, and filed for divorce. It was time to end the marriage once and for all—by law.

After I was able to process the events I'd gone through, I came to a clear decision on how I felt about mandatory helmet laws. I was 100 percent for them. They were completely necessary. I researched traumatic brain injuries (TBIs), and I discovered TBIs are a silent epidemic. In the United States there are two million new brain injuries every year. What surprised me was how easily they arose in simple ways like just falling (which accounts for almost half). Sadly, I found out that TBI patients are the most untreated and unemployable group of injured people in the world, and it ruins their lives. Since I was opening a new book of life, with blank chapters to fill, I made a commitment to help those trapped in this silent epidemic.

I went to a press conference at the Bonaventure Hotel in downtown Los Angeles. This time I told them my true feelings about what happened. I discussed my accident in detail, the injury, the brain surgery. I admitted that all the things I'd said just after the accident were wrong and urged all state legislatures to pass a helmet law that would prevent people from riding a motorcycle without a helmet. I said, "I don't have any tolerance for people who want to ride free in the wind. If you don't wear a helmet, you're not playing with a full deck."

On January 1, 1992, the helmet law in California went into effect.

Soon after the helmet law went into effect, my Harley-Davidson was stolen from my front yard. I have an idea who stole it—an angry motorcycle enthusiast neighbor of mine who was pissed off that he'd lost the helmet law battle. He attributed his loss to my help getting the helmet law passed. But that was fine by me. My tour on motorcycles was over.

Shortly after the press conference at the Bonaventure Hotel, President George Herbert Walker Bush invited me to the White House for a briefing with HUD, the United States Department of Housing and Urban Development. I told them about the accident and how it happened. I said, "The helmet law should be mandatory in all states; we have to have something to protect the people. If I had been wearing a helmet, this wouldn't have happened." Parts of what we discussed at the briefing became the initial language used to create the federal Traumatic Brain Injury Act, which President Bill Clinton signed on July 29, 1996. The legislation was the only federal program focused on issues faced by individuals and families with traumatic brain injuries, which provides for treatment and tracking of this silent epidemic on a national level.

At first, I had a great deal of regret regarding the accident, but my misfortune brought awareness to head injuries, which helped create a law that assists many people every day, even now. That gave me a really good feeling. I thank my angels every day for allowing me to give back in that way. I turned my mess into a message. What I want people to take from my experience is: If you choose to Rollerblade, ski, skateboard, or ride a bicycle or a motorcycle without wearing a helmet, you're challenging the face of death. It's a gamble you're bound to lose sooner or later, like I did. When the odds catch up with you, that fate will snatch your life and break the hearts of everyone who loves you.

33. FREEDOM

Facing Real Exciting Energy
Developing Outta Miracles

THE YEAR FOLLOWING THE MOTORCYCLE ACCI-
DENT was very busy for me professionally. I did five
movies back to back. Among those were two of my most
popular, *Predator 2* and *Point Break*. I had no problem
memorizing lines, as one might imagine after brain surgery.
Going back to work was second nature; I just picked up
right where I left off.

Whenever I start a new job, my biggest highlight is getting to know the cast and crew. It's like inheriting a new
supportive, loving family. The cast and crew on *Point Break*
were more than a family to me; they were like members of a
tribe. Being Native American, I know the power of a tribe,
and the *Point Break* tribe was unstoppable.

Working with our incredible leader, Kathryn Bigelow,
was an answer to my prayers. For a long time, I'd prayed to
work with a female director. I knew a story coming from the
heart of a woman would be very powerful and filled with
details and emotion. I was correct. Kathryn had an incredible ability to connect with the artist and make things

With Patrick Swayze. (*Courtesy of Jeff Kravitz / Filmmagic.com*)

happen with ease. She adhered to the formula of a good script but still allowed the unexpected. Sometimes in rehearsals, I added dialogue. Kathryn loved and supported my improvisations. A lot of my improvised dialogue ended up in the movie and have become favorites lines that fans still quote, like, "Utah! Get me two."

Most of my scenes were with Keanu Reeves. I was very impressed with his eagerness and openness to grow as an artist. He was young, yet his ability to perform and understand details was right on target. When I met Patrick Swayze, I found out we were both from Harris County, Texas, which gave us a special bond. We both felt a soul mate connection with a familiar feeling like we had already known each other. Although we didn't have many scenes together, our friendship grew very strong.

The *Point Break* tribe worked flawlessly together. Usually when I reflect on a movie, I think, *I wish I could change this* or *Ooh, I could have done that.* That never happened on *Point Break;* it was an immaculate production. The wrap party was very upbeat and congratulatory. I don't remember where it was held, but I can picture the packed room filled with three hundred proud people celebrating the great work they had accomplished. We all knew we had just completed something extremely special.

At the party, Patrick (for reasons unknown) slipped in front of me to tell me about the pleasures of skydiving, then slipped away and disappeared. Surprisingly, he did this about a dozen times, each time describing in detail how amazing skydiving is. He continued his little game until finally, he spun me around, got real serious, looked me dead in the eyes, and said in that confident Swayze tone, "I'm going to take you; you'll enjoy it."

"Okay, fine, I'll go." The words slipped out of my mouth before I could stop them, and we shook hands. I didn't *mean* it. I had no intention of actually jumping out of a perfectly good airplane. I just said okay to shut him up.

Patrick beamed with excitement. "You're gonna love it! This is the best thing you can do to liberate your freedom."

I didn't think more about it. I had no intention of going. Then, a few minutes later, a crew member approached me grinning. "So I hear you're going skydiving with Patrick."

The next day, Patrick called me. "Here's what's going to happen—you'll come to my house at 4:30 in the morning. I'll drive us to Perris Valley, you'll go through ground school, then you'll do your first jump."

I still didn't want to go. However, as planned, I arrived at Patrick's ranch house in Sunland, California, at 4:30 A.M., just as the sun was rising. Wide-awake Patrick was waiting for me outside by his two white Arabian horses. He drove us two hours to Perris Valley just outside of Riverside. Patrick talked about skydiving the whole time.

We arrived at a barren strip of desert land. I didn't know what to expect; I had no idea what the requirements were to make me qualified to jump out of an airplane at thirteen thousand feet.

The instructors took me into a room with video monitors on the wall and handed me twelve sheets of paper to sign. Each sheet had multiple paragraphs to initial, telling me how many different ways I could be killed, what could be maimed on my body, and that they were *not liable* for anything that happened to me.

"Don't read this; it's bullshit. Just sign it," Patrick interjected. Even before filming *Point Break,* Patrick was a big skydiver and an incredible athlete and dancer. I trusted him. I signed the papers and immediately started ground school.

Ground school took six hours. In those six hours, two jumpmasters taught me everything: the correct posture, when to jump, how to jump, various hand signals, what to do with my arms and legs. Over and over, we practiced jumping. Patrick watched me, smirking the whole time.

After ground school, I boarded a small silver Twin Otter plane with Patrick and about fifteen other guys. We sat on the floor of the plane and rode thirty minutes to our jump altitude of thirteen thousand feet. When we reached thirteen thousand feet, the door of the plane opened over our drop zone. I suddenly forgot everything I had just practiced. I felt paralyzed. I imagine my face looked like a hood ornament, frozen and pale. The other guys sported looks of terror on their faces as well. Patrick, on the other hand, was beaming the same perpetually happy grin that I had grown to love. He was the first person to jump. When Patrick got to the door, just before jumping, he said, "When you get to this door and look out, you will face fear and apprehension like you have never faced before. Don't think. Just remember the three words. 'Ready. Set. *Go!*' And jump." He sprang out the door shouting, "See you at the bottom!" I watched him free-fall, doing little ballet pirouettes in the air like he did in *Point Break*. One by one, every other diver jumped out of the plane. As it got close to my turn, I couldn't even remember those three vital words.

"Ready, set, go," the jumpmaster reminded me.

As the Twin Otter cut through the air going eighty-five miles per hour, I stood at the open door, looking down. Just as Patrick warned, I was filled with fear. *Don't think*, I told myself. "Ready, set, *go!*" I shouted, and I leaped out of the plane.

Plummeting into the abyss of nothingness at 120 mph, I began free-falling like a rock with my jumpmaster beside me. I hurtled nine thousand feet in fifty-five seconds. My face felt like a rubber puppet flipping and flapping against my head. The free fall was incredible. It was everything that Patrick had described and more. For that short time in the air, I felt a freedom I had never imagined possible. In the middle of my reverie, the jumpmaster gave me the "pull your rip cord" signal. Engrossed in my moment of complete freedom, I found it hard to believe the time had come to pull the cord. I checked my altimeter, and I was at twenty-five hundred feet. I pulled the rip cord. With the parachute open, I floated in the air like a butterfly for fifteen minutes. My body felt no resistance to anything, like an angel hovering over the earth in complete bliss.

First, I landed on my feet, and then on my butt. With great energy swirling inside of me, I howled, "That was great! Better than sex!" Everyone had already taken their chutes off and were running toward me, screaming and shouting, peppering me with questions.

"What did you think? How did it feel?"

I was speechless.

Patrick approached and put his arm around me. "You did great. I knew you would be good at it."

"Thanks, man. I am so honored you chose to share this with me." I gave him a bear hug. "Can I do it again?"

"No."

Patrick became my skydiving mentor. We took a total of eight trips together until one day I felt I had done as many jumps as I needed to. I let the skydiving tour go down in history, and as I always do, I moved on to my next project, a better man than I was before. Patrick forced me to face the fear in the caves of my mind with a flashlight. I will always have Patrick's skydiving message of freedom inside of me.

Years after Patrick's death, I was sitting outside of my house on a bench looking out at the ocean. It was a nice, beautiful day—not too hot, not too cold, clear skies—when out of nowhere came Patrick Swayze's spirit flying right above me twenty feet from my head, and right behind him was my father's spirit. I know they came from the spiritual realm to reveal to me their love and freedom.

34. DRAG

Don't Refuse A Girl

IN 1992, I continued my professional run with another blockbuster action thriller, *Under Siege*, opposite Steven Seagal and Tommy Lee Jones, playing another bad guy. My character, Commander Krill, was a rogue mercenary who kills his captain to seize a U.S. battleship. The movie was shot at the USS *Alabama* Battleship Memorial Park in Mobile, on a retired ship that had actually been in combat during World War II. It was incredible the way Frank Tidy, our director of photography, made the museum ship look like it was out to sea to portray our ship, the USS *Missouri*. With my first step onto the ship, my artistic juices began flowing. I already felt at home; the ship became my best friend. I drew on the military upbringing I'd endured to fuel Commander Krill's life inside of me.

The director, Andy Davis, gave me a book about the USS *Missouri* going to combat in the Persian Gulf War. "If you have any ideas, give 'em to me," he said. It was a captivating read. I was particularly fascinated by the part about "Pollywog Day." This was when the ship crossed the equator and all the first-year soldiers (known as Pollywogs or 'Wogs) who had never crossed the equator before spent one day being hazed by Shellbacks (soldiers who had already crossed the equator). It was a way that first-year sailors were tested for their seaworthiness before they became Shellbacks.

The Shellbacks did flagrant things to the first-year sailors. They forced them to drink coffee made out of seawater, smeared them with garbage and rotten food. Some first-year soldiers were even beaten. They called this "the Ceremony of Crossing the Line." Not only did the ceremony involve those brazen challenges, it also included a cross-dressing beauty contest where the winner was labeled "Queen of the Wogs." As I read about this audacious tradition, I had incredible visions of how my character could kill the captain.

Excited, I found Andy immediately. "You said if I had any ideas to give them to you, so here's the idea: I want to kill the captain . . . in drag."

"What?"

"I'm gonna dress up like the Queen of the Wogs in female wardrobe, and I'm gonna kill the captain."

"What?" Andy stared at me, mystified.

"It's right here in the book." I had the page bookmarked. I showed it to him. "It's a ritual. Don't worry; I'll make it authentic."

Andy gave the book a quick gander. "Okay, I'll run it by the studio."

"Great!"

I started to get myself ready for my big debut as a woman. I had wardrobe get me a 44DD stuffed bra, a short, pleated blue skirt just below my knees, and a short-sleeved white blouse with blue polka dots. I used my own socks, my own navy shoes, and my own underwear. To finish off the look, I secured a Tina Turner wig. The plan was brilliant; nothing could stop me. I was artistically charged to the max. I visited Steven Seagal in his big Winnebago parked in

Under Siege, 1992. (Licensed by Warner Bros. Entertainment, Inc. All Rights Reserved.)

the fields of Mobile to tell him my idea. He asked whose idea it was. I told him it was mine. His reaction was not what I expected; it was bland and cold. Then I decided to run it by Tommy Lee Jones. He loved it. *"Do it!"* He laughed.

The next day, I found out the studio had rejected my idea. Their reasoning was something to the effect that they were making a Steven Seagal martial arts movie, not a movie about Gary Busey in drag. I understood their hesitation, but I was not going to give up. I almost expected the rejection after my talk with Steven. However, with my commitment to creating the most entertaining and authentic characters possible, I knew I could find a way to make this happen. I told the studio, "I'll have both genders done before lunch, and you can make your choice. I promise I won't go overtime, and it won't cost anything extra."

The studio agreed.

I did it twice—once as Commander Krill the male and

once as Nancy Krill the female. I named her Nancy because her favorite song was "Rocky Raccoon" from the Beatles. After I did Nancy's take, Tommy Lee Jones laughed so hard he couldn't stand up. It was all done before lunch as promised. A few weeks later, Andy approached me with a grin. "The woman's in," he announced. The studio chose the female version.

I was elated. It was a feeling of artistic victory. Creating Nancy Krill was a great lesson of artistic persistence and trust of the divine inspirations that come from that feeling way down in your gut.

Sometime after we wrapped, I got a call from Tommy Lee Jones. When I answered, he was laughing. "I just can't stop laughing thinking about you as a woman."

"Want a date?" I asked.

"How can I refuse?"

Under Siege, 1992, with Tommy Lee Jones. (*Licensed by Warner Bros. Entertainment, Inc. All Rights Reserved.*)

The Firm, with Sydney Pollack. *(© Paramount Pictures Corp. All Rights Reserved. Courtesy of Paramount Pictures.)*

35. DREAM

Details Revealing
Excitement And Magic

IN 1993, I was in Chicago filming a family movie called
Rookie of the Year. Out of the blue, I got a call from the
incredible director Sydney Pollack. He said, "Remember
when you said it was a dream of yours to work together?
Well, I have a part for you. I need you in Memphis, Tennessee, for a movie."

"Great! What's it called?"

"*The Firm.*"

"Is it about plastic surgery?" We both chuckled.

"No, it's that bestselling book by John Grisham, with
Tom Cruise and Jeanne Tripplehorn."

I'd known Jeanne since she was eight years old. I used to
play music with her father in Tulsa. "What's the part?"

"You'll be playing a private detective in a scene with Tom
Cruise and Holly Hunter." Sydney's excitement about the
movie was contagious. This was sounding like a dream come
true.

"Let's do it! When do you need me?"

"In three days."

"I've got two more weeks on this movie in Chicago."

Our excitement deflated. Sydney sighed, then said, "Okay, we'll do it another time. Talk to you later. Bye."

Dial tone.

There was a pang in my heart. I had been waiting almost fifteen years for an invitation from Sydney to work with him. I'd met Sydney on an airplane in 1980. We were both on our way to visit Willie Nelson in Austin, Texas, and coincidentally sat next to each other in first class. Sydney was producing a movie starring Willie called *Honeysuckle Rose,* and I was just going for a visit.

I spent the week with Willie, playing music, having fun watching him work on *Honeysuckle Rose* (which was humorously dubbed *Honey, Suck My Rose*), and getting to know Sydney. Sydney and I carried a mutual respect for each other. I respected him as an astonishing filmmaker, and he respected me as an accomplished actor. I told him, "It's a dream of mine to work with you."

"Someday we will," Sydney agreed.

That someday had finally arrived, and I wasn't free! I couldn't help feeling that I was missing out on something very magical. Then, surprisingly, during the final week of filming *Rookie of the Year,* I got another call from Sydney. "Hey, listen, we've changed our schedule to fit yours; I'll need you for three days in Memphis, Tennessee. When can you be here?"

A week later, just after I wrapped in Chicago, I went to Memphis to work on *The Firm.* Working with Sydney was in fact a dream come true. He masterfully had everything lined up in such great detail (the measurements, lighting, angles, lenses) that the actors didn't have to think about anything except being free. All I had to do was follow his

The Firm, with Tom Cruise and Holly Hunter.
(© Paramount Pictures Corp. All Rights Reserved.
Courtesy of Paramount Pictures.)

direction and let the magic unfold. In my first scene, Mitch McDeere, portrayed by Tom Cruise, recruits my character's services to help him find out who is killing lawyers around town. Tom had maybe two lines, but Sydney gave me a very specific and unexpected direction. He said, "Don't let Tom speak. Use that Busey energy to shut him down. You're talking about a truck driver named Elvis, mixing coffee with Sweet'N Low, but when Tom tries to speak, interrupt him any way you can. *Don't let him get a line in.*"

When I met Tom on the set, I got the feeling that he was ready for anything. He always had an excited smile on his face that was infectious. Tom had that special ability to make anyone he spoke with feel like he or she was the most important person on the planet. He made me feel like doing this scene with me was the greatest thing that ever happened to him. Of course I know it wasn't, but that was Tom's magic—making people feel special. Getting Sydney's secret direction made me feel like we were playing a joke on Tom, which was very fun. I knew in order for this to work, I had only one chance to surprise Tom. I said my lines about Elvis the truck driver rapid-fire, like a machine gun, blasting through Tom's lines. He had no chance to get in a word. The scene turned out great. We did it in one take.

In my next scene, Holly Hunter and I are making out just before two thugs burst into my office and ultimately shoot and kill me. Holly, being a committed and courageous actress, wanted to rehearse, so we made out for twenty minutes. When it came time to film, Sydney, who was always a whole day ahead of everyone else, explained the scene. I was going to be shot four times. He showed me with meticulous detail how to take each shot: in the earlobe, forearm, chest, and stomach. Because of Sydney's precision in directing me, I did it in one take again. It was beautiful. My movie experience with Sydney made me realize dreams really do come true.

36. SOUL

Showing Others Unconditional Love

IN 1993, my friend Jeff Bridges invited me to visit him in San Francisco where he was filming the movie *Fearless*. It was about a guy who survived a terrible plane crash. Jeff wanted me to share with him the details of my motorcycle accident so he could understand what it felt like to experience a near-death encounter. I was more than happy to give my knowledge to him; our friendship is based on giving.

I met Jeff in 1972 on my first big movie with MGM called *The Lolly-Madonna War,* shot in Knoxville, Tennessee. The movie was similar to a Hatfield-and-McCoy situation between two families feuding over a maid. Jeff and I played sons of opposing families. I'd already known of Jeff before I'd met him. He was just coming off the huge hit movie *The Last Picture Show,* and of course I knew of his famous father, Lloyd Bridges, from the television show *Sea Hunt* among many of his hit television shows and movies.

Meeting Jeff for the first time took me by surprise. I looked into his eyes and felt like I could see his soul. Everything about him seemed so familiar to me, like I knew him from before. Because he felt so familiar to me, the enterprise of communication came very naturally. We weren't trying to figure out what to talk about; it always just flowed. I was struck by how loving and giving Jeff's nature was. We were kindred spirits sharing similar interests, especially in music. We became great friends really fast over the three-month shoot.

On set during our downtime, we thought of different shenanigans we could embark on to entertain ourselves and the crew. One day while we were working in the backwoods of Tennessee around a corral, there was an old Fresca can that people had been using to hock loogies, spit chewing tobacco, and throw cigarettes butts in, hanging on a post. The can was full. I picked it up and pretended I was gonna drink it. Jeff said, "How much would it cost for you to drink that?"

"I don't know; make me an offer."

He started the bidding at one dollar, then the crew chimed in, "Two bucks . . . three bucks . . . four bucks . . . five bucks . . ." Finally, it got to twelve bucks. I grabbed the Fresca can and chugalugged. It felt like I was drinking worms and bugs with mucus. Before the contents made their way down, I puked all over myself. Jeff, along with the crew, were rolling on the ground roaring with laughter. They were so entertained by my lunacy they gave me an extra four bucks, making it a whopping total of sixteen dollars—plus vomit.

I never lived that one down.

After *Lolly-Madonna,* Jeff became my best friend in the industry. We hung out constantly, playing music and doing creative things together. Jeff became "Uncle Jeff" to my two-year-old son, Jake. I became friendly with his family,

Making music with Jeff Bridges, 2010.
(Courtesy of Steffanie Sampson)

too. In my heart, they felt like my West Coast family. Ironically, the next movie I was cast in, *The Last American Hero,* was with Jeff again; this time we played brothers. It felt so real to play his brother because in my mind he *was* my brother.

During the filming, we always had our guitars with us. We referred to our guitars as our therapists. Jeff's was Dr. Martin, and mine was Dr. Gibson (Jeff had a Martin guitar, and I had a Gibson guitar). One day on the set, deep in the woods of North Carolina, we forgot our guitars. We couldn't survive without them, so we had a teamster drive sixty miles through the woods to our hotel to retrieve them. Playing music together was a warm symphony of communication between our hearts. Doing that movie imprinted a deep brotherly love in my soul that is just as strong now as it was then.

Jeff was a very generous person, always sharing his knowledge and assisting me in the industry. After *The Last American Hero,* he helped me earn a part in the movie *Thunderbolt and Lightfoot,* directed by Clint Eastwood. One day, when I was feeling impatient with how slowly things were happening for me, I asked Jeff, "What's it going to take for me to have the power that you do to be cast in movies all the time?"

He said matter-of-factly, with unconditional love, "Boo-say [he often calls me *Boo-say,* or *Boose* (rhymes with *goose*)], it's just a matter of time. Be patient, relax, don't try to push it." A lightbulb went off, and I got a feeling of relief. *Ahh, it's going to happen; I just have to wait for the time to come.*

When Jeff asked me to visit him on the set of *Fearless,* it was my pleasure to return the favor. What people don't know is that I crashed my motorcycle on Jeff Bridges's birthday, December 4, further bonding us into brotherhood. Jeff flew me up to San Francisco. I described my near-death experience to him in detail: leaving my body, being surrounded by angels, getting information from the other side. Then I explained, "You know what it's like, Jeff? It's like you're an angel in an earth suit."

He bent over backward, laughing, repeating the words, "An angel in an earth suit!"

"Yeah, that's what I am, because I was there. My soul was there. Your character in the movie is going to be there, too. All you have to do is feel that angelic power inside of you. Everything is unconditional love and harmony there, and that's what it feels like."

Jeff asked me to bless the movie. We sat down in a circle, took each other's hands, and called Jeff's angels and spiritual guides to be with him and give him the feeling that he was an angel in an earth suit. From that time on, he flew fearless and free.

With Jeff Bridges in 2009.
(Courtesy of Steffanie Sampson)

Predator 2 (© 1990 Twentieth Century Fox. All Rights Reserved.)

37. RELAPSE

Really Exciting Love Affair
Perfecting Self-Extermination

B Y JUNE OF 1994, I was back at the top of my game. My career was in full swing. The list of big-budget block-busters went on and on—*Lethal Weapon, Predator 2, Point Break, Under Siege, Rookie of the Year, The Firm, Surviving the Game, Drop Zone*. I was also enjoying the freedom that came with my new bachelor lifestyle—going from movie to movie, socializing at parties without any anchors weighing me down. My biggest accomplishment was that I had been sober from cocaine for nine years—ever since the day I'd said that angry prayer driving out of my neighborhood in Malibu West. Cocaine was part of my distant past, never to return again. I did not waste a single thought on cocaine.

One particular night, I was at a big Hollywood party when a provocative girl from across the room caught my eye. She smiled seductively, then sashayed toward me. She spoke in a Danish accent, which was intriguing. There was definite chemistry. We sat down to kiss next to a big round table where I noticed a large oval-shaped plate loaded with

Drop Zone, with Wesley Snipes. *(© Paramount Pictures Corp. All Rights Reserved. Courtesy of Paramount Pictures.)*

cocaine, as big as a Sunday steak dinner in Texas.

I stared at that plate of cocaine for two hours. The little white mountains of cocaine glimmered like diamonds. They called to me, like sirens luring a nearby sailor with enchanting music. Soon, the plate became more attractive than the hot Danish girl. Then my long-lost addicted counterpart crawled out of the darkness to taunt me. "You've been sober so long it's not a problem anymore. Try a little bit. Prove to yourself you have control. It won't affect you the way it used to. You're over it. *You deserve a reward!*" Quickly I realized my addict was right . . . I *had* been sober a long time, it *wasn't* a problem anymore, *I definitely deserved a reward!*

I gave the Danish girl a big smooch on the lips, then feverishly grabbed the razor blade from the table, scraped the powder into three straight lines, yanked a hundred-dollar bill from my pocket, rolled it up, and vacuumed the three lines like a Black + Decker industrial Dustbuster. *Whoosh!* It was like a hook came out of the darkness and yanked me out of the light. I didn't question the yanking; I went with it.

38. STRIPPER

Standing Tall Revealing Intimate
Private Parts Expecting Remuneration

B Y LATE 1994, cocaine made its way back into my daily
life; so did football. Coming from Texas, I was a huge
fan of the Dallas Cowboys. I flew to Dallas to watch them
play every weekend when they were in town. I became a fix-
ture on the sidelines. I got to know the Cowboys very well. I
went to practice with them, hung out in the locker room,
and socialized with them.

While I was in Dallas, some friends took me, for my first
time, to a gentlemen's club called Cabaret Royale. We sat
at a large table in front of a U-shaped stage where half-
naked girls pranced around posing in the smoky pinkish-
purple light. Immediately, a group of giggling, scantily clad
young ladies sauntered over and gave me a quick little jig as
they joined the ladies romping onstage. My friends invited
a young woman dressed in normal street clothes to join us
at our table. She took the only seat available—next to me.
She was beautiful; her hazel eyes shimmered against her olive skin and raven hair. She carried a beguiling vibration

that attracted me. We struck up a conversation that flowed from topic to topic. Then she said, "I work here."

"What do you do here?" I asked.

"I dance." I did not expect that! But I continued to enjoy her company—even though she was on the job—until we left.

The next season, I was on the sidelines again. I also found myself at another gentlemen's club called the Men's Club with my friends. As we settled into the best booth in the house, I noticed a dancer donning a lavender see-through top staring at me from thirty feet away. I immediately recognized her; she was the exotic dancer in street clothes I'd met the year before. I called her over. The instant she sat down, I felt a calibration of feelings spinning on the edge of the unknown. Her name was Tiani. We spent the whole night together talking and laughing, getting to know each other. When I left, she didn't ask for payment, and I didn't offer any. Instead, I invited her to join me later at a popular club called Sipango's when she got off work.

Sipango's, an upscale club with good food, live music, dancing, *and clothes*, was more my style. To my surprise, Tiani met me there after she got off work. There was something electric between us; we spent the night dancing and drinking. Afterward, I took her back to my hotel, where we spent the night joined at the hip like raw, explosive animals. She had the most remarkable moves in bed, each one like a brand-new heaven I'd never experienced. I quickly became bewitched by her spell. After our night together, I had to be with her all the time; she became my long-distance girlfriend.

Once word got out that we were an item, I received a call from a close friend in Dallas warning me, "Don't get mixed up with that stripper girl; she's a drinker and a drug taker who will cling to anyone that will buy her liquor." That might have been true, but it didn't matter; I was already in too deep. In my mind, we were soul mates. I knew my love was going to change her. She was merely a young woman trying to make it on her own after a terrible upbringing in a broken home. I ignored the warning.

My relationship with Tiani was on an accelerated course, moving as fast as lightning. I brought her into my world. She yearned to be an actress in the movies, so I got her parts in my movies. The first part was in a movie called *The Rage* in Park City, Utah. She did as well as she could; her acting was like a twelve-year-old girl looking in the mirror making faces and saying funny things. But I knew with training she'd get good. She enrolled in acting classes, which helped her improve immensely. With a little technique, she was a natural. The next movie I got her was *The Chain*. Everything was rolling along smoothly until I received a letter from Belinda.

You see, Belinda and I had rekindled our romance after I'd recovered from the motorcycle accident and gotten divorced. We were together for a couple of years, but I was too intense for her. She pulled away, and ultimately, our romance fizzled. I had spent the last two years trying to get over her. Seeing Belinda's handwriting on the envelope made my heart soar. I tore the letter open. Inside was a magazine clipping of Belinda in one of her modeling shots with *Please give me a second chance. Love, Belinda* written on it. I was surprised, excited, and confused. I knew in my heart Belinda and I belonged together, but the timing didn't feel right. I was back on drugs and in a relationship with a stripper. I didn't respond. I have always regretted not listening to the truth of my pure heart.

39. SIN

Self-Imposed Nonsense

I N MAY OF 1995, I was still in a relationship with Tiani, who no longer danced for a living. I visited her almost every week in Dallas for an indulgently good time. While in Dallas I experimented with a new drug called GHB—also known as G, Gina, or Liquid Ecstasy. Tiani boasted that it would turn up our sexual desires for each other. Never one to say no to drugs, I took the recommended dose, *one teaspoon*. She wasn't kidding; on GHB, sex was incredible.

On Wednesday, May 3, 1995, I brought Tiani *and* a container of GHB home from Dallas. Back in Malibu, our plan for the night was to go to the House of Blues in Hollywood to watch friends play music. I did some coke, then went to the bathroom to get ready for our night out, but I got sidetracked when I noticed Tiani had left the bottle of GHB on the counter. Like a sneaky child, I quietly slipped into the kitchen, retrieved a spoon, then slithered back to the bathroom, where I took *two tablespoons* of the drug. Feeling incredible, I went outside on my back patio, with a view overlooking the vast Pacific Ocean, to watch the sunset. As I admired the intense, bold, crimson colors in the sky, I took a deep breath of fresh ocean air, then *collapsed*.

When I regained consciousness, it took me a moment to realize that I was on an operating table with my arms stretched out as if on a cross. I couldn't move my body or open my eyes. It felt like I couldn't breathe, but somehow I did. It took a moment for me to register there was a large tube, two inches wide, shoved down my throat, sucking everything out from what felt like every orifice: the food I had eaten, everything I'd drunk, all the stuff I'd snorted. There was liquid coming out of my mouth, my nose, and my eyes. Gas was seeping out of me, urine, and liquid stains of who knows what. Although I couldn't talk, my mind was very alert; I could hear, and I could think. My thought was, *I might go now. This might be the end.* I felt death coming for me just around the corner. *What a stupid way to go,* I thought. It was the first time in my life that I felt death was a possibility. Instantly, I was flooded with regret for being so foolish, indulgent, reckless, and for imposing this torture upon myself.

Then I felt a very intense rush of power in my lower abdomen that came with the feeling, *You're going to be fine.* It was like I had the devil on one shoulder representing death and an angel on the other representing life. I chose to focus on the angel. I surrendered, relaxed, and let the doctors continue pumping out all the dung I'd chosen to put inside of my body. I have no idea how long they pumped my stomach; it didn't matter. I acquiesced to the apparatus working inside of me saving my life. With every pulse, every sound, I affirmed it was helping me. I knew *faith* would be the power that would heal me. Then I heard a doctor say,

"He'll recover." When the machines stopped sucking the poison I'd polluted myself with, the doctor leaned over my limp body to reassure me, "Gary, you're past the bad part. Just take it easy; we're giving you something to sedate you. You'll be staying in the hospital tonight."

I slept hard that night. I was out like a candle in a windy storm. The next day, I felt extreme pain in my stomach, esophagus, neck, and face (like someone took a toilet plunger, put it down my mouth, and went *whoop whoop whoop*). I was relieved to feel the pain; I was still alive. I felt like I had a new life where I could start fresh *again*.

That overdose was like a two-by-four slamming me hard in the head to get my attention. It took near death, for a second time, to wake me up. The cocaine years were the time I spent dancing with the devil, but the devil was always leading the dance. I realized I had been living in the darkest of nights all day long with cocaine. Recovering in the hospital, I simply decided, *I'm not doing this anymore*. I moved out of the circle I'd been dancing in and left that self-imposed nonsense behind me forever.

40. SOBER

Son Of a Bitch Everything's Real

AFTER THE DRUG OVERDOSE, I spent four days in the hospital recovering. When I was released, I got news that I would be facing felony drug possession charges, which held a possible sentence of three years in prison. Because the doctor found cocaine in my shirt pocket while saving my life, the police acquired a court order to search my house. They found a half gram of cocaine, four grams of marijuana, and two grams of hallucinogenic mushrooms. Luckily, when I went to court, the judge was lenient. Since I had no criminal record, he ordered me to undergo a twenty-eight-day drug-treatment program at Charter Hospital in Cathedral City, California. Once it was completed, all the drug charges would be dropped.

Even though I was forced into the treatment program at Charter Hospital, I welcomed the change. It felt good to be taken out of society, out of the cocaine-riddled world of destruction I'd created, and placed into a new world of order and responsibility. The hospital became a safe place of relaxation, comfort, meditation, and prayer. It was a time for meticulously uncovering the reality of the derelict I had become and the magnitude of my degeneracy. I felt like I had been swimming in a filthy pool that hadn't been cleaned for fifty years with smoky bubbles of gas, animal bones, and muffled cries of help rising to the surface. Even though instinctively I knew it was bad to swim there, I had done it for so long I didn't even see the filth anymore. At Charter Hospital, I finally pulled the plug on the mental debris floating in my filthy pool and let it drain, to expose all the garbage, twigs, weeds, ziplock bags, straws, broken glass, and razor blades that had accumulated in my mind so I could finally change. I was ready to be rigorously honest with myself.

My daily routine comprised therapy, menial chores, medication, and twelve-step meetings. In fact, I went to twelve-step meetings three times a day, where they shoveled new information into my brain. This was my first time in therapy. Initially, I was diagnosed with manic-depressive disorder (bipolar) and subsequently treated for that with medication. Then, after further counseling, the diagnosis changed to attention deficit disorder. Getting that diagnosis gave me great relief. Pushing everything out of the dark into the light set me at ease. I was finally being real with myself.

After twenty-eight enlightening days, I got out. On the outside, everything felt fresh, new, and exciting. I knew I was done with cocaine *forever*. I thanked God for the overdose. It finally got my attention once and for all. There was no doubt in my mind, I was finally free to lead a normal life.

The challenge I faced, when I got out of rehab, was that I was back with Tiani, who still consumed alcohol on a regular basis. It was like pouring gasoline on a fire. I knew I was too weak to have any substance abuse around me, so it became very important that she get sober, too. I was 100 percent committed to my new sobriety, and I couldn't be around temptations in any form—drugs or alcohol. At first, Tiani was resistant to the idea of sobriety, but four months into my sobriety, she got sober, too (for the first time since being a teenager). Together, our sobriety sparked an even deeper connection between us. I wanted her to be my wife. On Christmas Eve 1995, we got engaged.

When I announced our engagement, red flags started popping up. Multiple friends warned me not to marry her, including my Narcotics Anonymous sponsor, who advised me to wait at least two years while I rediscovered myself. But I chose to ignore everyone. For me, as always, it was full speed ahead. I hired the best wedding planner in Dallas to give my future bride the wedding of her dreams. I wanted her to have the full treatment. My fiancée never stopped smiling while we planned the wedding—bouncing around, slamming her hand on my thigh, always hugging and kissing me. I thought, *Wow, things couldn't be better! She is so loving!*

On September 23, 1996, with fourteen months of sobriety under my belt and ten months of sobriety under her belt, we celebrated the beginning of our new life together with a lavish wedding at the Morton H. Meyerson Symphony Center in Dallas. The celebration was attended by hundreds of guests, although many good friends and family members were noticeably absent (my son Jake included). Following our wedding was a luxurious two-week honeymoon at a private estate in Acapulco with an ocean view overlooking the island. My new bride kept walking around repeating, "I'm married now. We're married." She resembled a small child. Everything in her life was so new, and

Black Sheep, with David Spade. *(© Paramount Pictures Corp. All Rights Reserved. Courtesy of Paramount Pictures.)*

that excited her. There was a lot of press surrounding our wedding. Whenever anyone asked what her profession was, our answer was actress.

The first few months of our marriage were very loving. We were leading a nice, clean, sober lifestyle; not a trace of alcohol was allowed in our home. I was still enjoying great success in my career. I'd just completed a comedy called *Black Sheep.* It was incredibly fun and exciting for me to be acting in a comedy with the marvelously talented Chris Farley and David Spade. Things were moving along splendidly until my wife began having anxiety attacks. I took her to the hospital frequently, like an ambulance, with my hazard lights blinking, dodging between cars to get her there as fast as I could. I noticed she naturally carried anxious emotions beneath the surface. I could only surmise the attacks were caused by the drastic changes in her life: not drinking alco-

Black Sheep, with Chris Farley. *(© Paramount Pictures Corp. All Rights Reserved. Courtesy of Paramount Pictures.)*

hol, moving to California, becoming the wife of a movie star. I suppose it was all too much. The pool was too deep; she was drowning.

Soon, my wife began disappearing. She was home less and less. After some time, she finally admitted that she was drinking again. I began to see a dark side emerge within her.

In no time, our marriage began to unravel like a cheap rope.

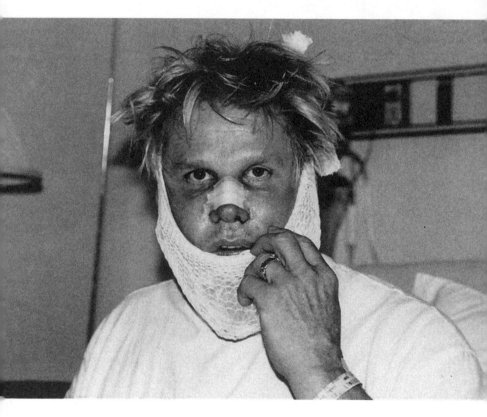

In the hospital after the cancer surgery.

41. FAITH

Fantastic Adventures
In Trusting *Him*

IN APRIL OF 1997, I was cast in a pilot reboot of an old television show called *Hawaii Five-0*. I often heard Hawaii brought out the best, or worst, in relationships, so I decided to bring my wife with me for the two-week shoot on the island of Oahu. I hoped that being in such a beautiful place together could rekindle even the slightest ember of love between us.

Unfortunately, most nights my wife ended up in a club ten blocks from our hotel where she drank with a castmate of mine until she passed out cold. Night after night, I picked her up off the floor, cleaned her up, and put her to bed. Having been sober for almost two years now, I could see clearly the writing on the wall. She was exactly as my friend had warned—a drinker who clung to anyone that would buy her liquor. I quickly realized my hope to reconnect would never happen. Having her around in Hawaii was bleeding me dry of artistic freedom and expression. I couldn't wait to end this experience.

On the final day of filming, everything flowed without a hitch until the last scene. My nose started bleeding. The medic on set tried to stop the nosebleed, but after an hour passed and the blood continued to gush, he called the paramedics. When the paramedics arrived, familiar with my work, they took great care of me. After trying multiple techniques to stop the bleeding, including stuffing my nose with cotton, placing a clamp on the bridge of my nose, and wedging gauze under my lip, they finally had to cauterize a spot inside my nose, which seemed to do the trick.

The next day, when we returned home to Malibu, everything seemed fine. I considered the nosebleed a fluke, something in the past, so I didn't bother to see a doctor about it. I went on with life as usual. Then, at the movies with my wife, I had another nosebleed. It was bad. We left the movie theater at the Third Street Promenade in Santa Monica to go home, but on the way out my wife met a group of people and stopped to talk to them. With blood gushing from my nose, I didn't have the patience to chat with strangers. I said, "Come on, let's go."

"You go on, I'm gonna hang with them for a bit." And so as I bled all over myself on the street, I watched my wife take off with her new friends.

At home I got the bleeding to stop using the techniques I learned from the paramedics in Hawaii. I slept well that night, but when I woke up in the morning, my nose gushed blood again. I quickly got my things together, and grabbed towels, tissue, and two disposable coffee cups to bleed into. As I was heading out the door to see my doctor, my wife was coming in after a night out with her new pals. I don't remember exactly what we said to each other in passing, but

I do remember telling her I was going to the doctor while bleeding into the coffee cup. She didn't offer to join me.

I drove myself to my general doctor, Scott Bateman in Malibu, expecting a quick fix, but he couldn't get the bleeding to stop. He said, "I want you to see a great ENT that I know in West LA named Chester Griffiths."

I was completely shocked that Dr. Bateman was not going to give me my quick fix. "You mean you can't stop the bleeding?"

"You need a specialist—now!" Dr. Bateman booked an appointment with Dr. Griffiths for an hour later, and I was off.

Within the hour, I entered the waiting room of Dr. Griffiths's office, bleeding into my second disposable coffee cup. Panicked, I shouted, "Can somebody help me? I may be dying!" Quickly, I was ushered into an examining room. Dr. Griffiths entered the room with a very positive demeanor. He held the energy of a person who could accomplish anything he set his mind to. His smile, and the sound of his voice, calmed me down immediately and gave me courage. But even he couldn't get the bleeding to stop.

"We're going to have to do surgery."

Surgery? Now?

The idea of a quick fix in my mind had now been obliterated. A nurse from Dr. Griffiths's office drove me to the emergency room at Santa Monica Hospital, where Dr. Griffiths operated on me. I awoke from the surgery to find out that he had discovered a malignant tumor, almost as big as a golf ball, growing in the left cheek sinus and in the nasal cavity right below my eye and tear duct apparatus. The tumor was a form of cancer called synovial cell sarcoma in the maxillary sinus. Ironically, after years of cocaine use, it was unrelated. Dr. Griffiths had removed and biopsied part of the tumor, but now he had to remove the rest. The surgery was scheduled to take place in two days. My dad died from an inoperable malignant tumor in his brain at age fifty-five. Now here I was fifty-two, almost the same age, slapped in the face with a cancer diagnosis—*in the middle of my face*!

The UCLA doctor at Santa Monica Hospital wanted to remove my eye and nose in order to get all the cancer out, but Dr. Griffiths argued he could remove all the cancer by going in through my nose with a new technology using tiny cameras. I would be Dr. Griffiths's first patient using this new technology, but he assured me he could save my face. He didn't blink when he spoke to me, which gave me confidence.

I had two days to prepare myself for the surgery. Cancer is a very scary prospect already, but more so when it is in the middle of your face. The face is the first thing people see; it's what makes a first impression. Judy used to refer to my face as "your famous face." She would often say, "Use your famous face to get us a table," or "Use your famous face to get in the front of the line." My famous face—my livelihood, my life—was in jeopardy. I found myself in a thick cloak of invisible fear. I meditated. While in deep meditation, I said to myself, "Dear Lord, I am filled with *fear* at this time." Then I heard a voice in the back of my head say, *Replace the word* fear *with* faith. I started dissecting what fear and faith really meant to me. Answers started pouring into my consciousness. I became aware that fear is self-created in a world of negativity. I understood that I, along with most people, had gotten used to entertaining fear and

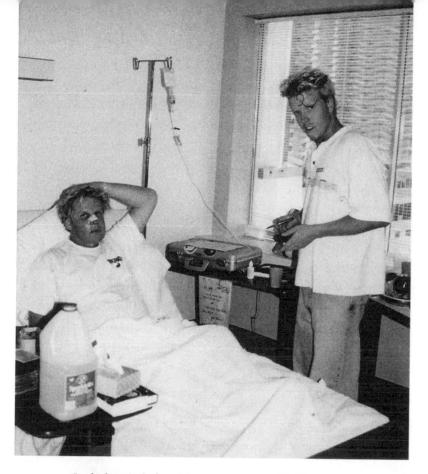

In the hospital after the cancer surgery with Jake Busey.

ignoring faith because the material world had become so convincing. Then a revelation came: The only reason I was in fear was because I was *not* in faith. If I stopped creating my fear, I could allow my faith to work for me at this dire time in my life. Faith was my only option; it was the difference between a good outcome and a bad outcome. Soon, instead of praying, "Dear Lord, I am filled with fear at this time," I found myself praying, "Dear Lord, I am filled with faith at this time." Instantly, I felt better. From that moment on, filled with faith, I *knew* everything would be fine. Faith was the biggest weapon I had. Faith allowed me to accept help from the invisible forces coming through the spiritual realm, the supernatural, my angels, my spiritual guides, and the creator at the central point of existence (who some people refer to as God).

I went into surgery knowing, with complete faith, that I had an excellent medical team and a legion of angels supporting me in my time of need. We were going to conquer this together. I don't remember if I was in pain when I awoke from the surgery, but I do remember I got an excited feeling because instinctively I knew the cancer was gone. I was correct; all the cancer had been removed, and my nose and eye were still intact. The surgery had been a complete success, as Dr. Griffiths had assured me it would be. I could go back to life as a healthy man.

With my hero, Dr. Chester Griffiths, 2018. *(Courtesy of Steffanie Sampson)*

42. BEAUTY

Be Exciting And Understanding
To Yourself

AFTER THE CANCER SURGERY, I recovered in the hospital for about a week. My son Jake and friend Tim Culbertson were constantly by my side. Tim, formerly Nick Nolte's double, became my double in 1995 and has been a good friend ever since. He was very generous to me while I was healing, constantly asking, "Is there anything you need?" My wife, on the other hand, was missing in action. I was so relieved that the cancer surgery was behind me, and a complete success, that I didn't care what she was doing. In my mind, the marriage was over. I planned to divorce her after I recovered (which I later did).

When Dr. Griffiths removed the bandages, I couldn't believe how swollen my head was, but my nose and my eye were intact. Dr. Griffiths was a miracle worker. If it hadn't been for him, my whole face would have been permanently disfigured. He assured me that once the swelling went down, I would look completely normal. I was so grateful to have him on my team, but he practiced otolaryngology, a surgical subspecialty that deals with conditions of the ear, nose, and throat, and since the tumor he removed was cancerous, I would now be in the hands of the oncologists on my team. They confirmed that every bit of *visible* cancer had in fact been removed. However, they warned me that there could be undetectable cancer roots and that I would have to undergo radiation therapy for six weeks. Initially, I didn't want to have radiation. Nothing in my heart felt right about having radiation, but the doctors were so convincing. They argued, "If there are cancer roots, you could get it again." I had to trust that the doctors were guiding me properly. I mean come on, *cancer in the middle of the face*! I was scared to death. I didn't know what to do.

Reluctantly, I agreed to have the radiation.

Over the next six weeks, I had radiation about twenty times. On a table, I lay with a gargantuan machine resembling a ball from outer space hovering over my head. It shot a red laser beam under my left eye for fifty-five seconds where the cancer had been. Then the laser beam moved to my right temple for eleven seconds, then to the left temple for eleven seconds. I didn't feel a thing. The whole treatment took about fifteen minutes. When the six-week radiation therapy was completed, I was told I could go on to live a normal life.

I can't really explain when it happened, because I don't understand the timing of it myself, but sometime after the radiation, maybe four weeks later, I caught a glimpse of myself in the mirror. A sick feeling deep in the pit of my stomach struck me. I looked horrible. I didn't recognize myself. The man I was looking at was not the same man I'd seen in the mirror for the past fifty-three years. The man in my reflection was a stranger with a crooked face. There was an abnormal pull on my face like a bad doll head. My left eye was yanked down and open more than the right one, and the left side of my nose was jerked up. The radiation disfigured my face.

I panicked. My famous face was ruined, messed up, and crooked. I spent a lot of time in the mirror lifting my nose to see if I could make it look better, pulling it up and down, adjusting my features, trying to make them look normal. No one had warned me radiation could distort my face. No one ever discussed any types of consequences or side effects—they must have been in the fine print somewhere—but I'm not a fine-print type of guy. I kicked myself. Why didn't I read the fine print? Why didn't I consult with Chester Griffiths before I'd had the radiation? Why was I always so careless? Then I realized blaming myself wasn't going to help me now. I had to stop beating myself up for not asking questions before having the radiation, stay strong, and find a way through this mess.

I found a plastic surgeon named Dr. Frank Ryan. I went to Dr. Ryan's office on Spaulding Avenue in Beverly Hills, filled with anxiety. I didn't know whether reconstructive surgery could be done or if it was applicable to what I was going through. My imagination ran wild. I wondered if I did have surgery, would there be scars? Would surgery make me look worse? Would I ever work again? I prayed Dr. Ryan could make it right. Upon arrival, I was ushered into Dr. Ryan's office right away. Walking down the hallway, I noticed pictures of dogs and horses hanging on the walls; for some reason, those pictures gave me a glimmer of comfort. Dr. Ryan, a smaller guy with a movie star face and hair cut perfectly short, entered his office and greeted me with a cheerful disposition.

"How can I help you?" he asked.

His embraceable demeanor relaxed me a bit. "I want to get my face evened up. Is there anything you can do?"

I showed him the different points on my face that were distorted and my ideas on how they could be corrected, again pulling various parts of my face up and down.

"I'm not sure. Let's see." Meticulously, he inspected my face. "Well, okay." He started getting creative, jotting down notes. "We can pull the left eye up a little, the left part of your nose up [which was my idea]. Yes, we can fix this."

I scheduled the surgery and left Dr. Ryan's office feeling very encouraged. The prospect of getting back to normal excited me.

On August 12, 1998, I had the surgery. After the surgery, I had to wait two long days to find out what my fate would be. When the time came. Dr. Ryan removed the bandages and said, "You're swollen, but that's normal. Wanna see?"

He handed me a mirror. I said a silent prayer, then looked at myself. I saw my familiar face looking back at me in the purity I was born with and had grown up with. Even through the swelling, I could tell my face was fixed. I looked like me again. Once the swelling went down, it was 99 percent normal. There are still a few reminders of my ordeal. My left eye is a little more open than the other . . . but that's the beauty of it.

Dr. Ryan and I lived on the same street in Malibu and became great friends after the surgery. Each of us, in his own way, made the other laugh automatically. We had fun on our excursions together, and I took him to a lot of movie premieres and concerts. On August 16, 2010, he tragically died in a car accident on Pacific Coast Highway; he is now an angel in the spiritual realm.

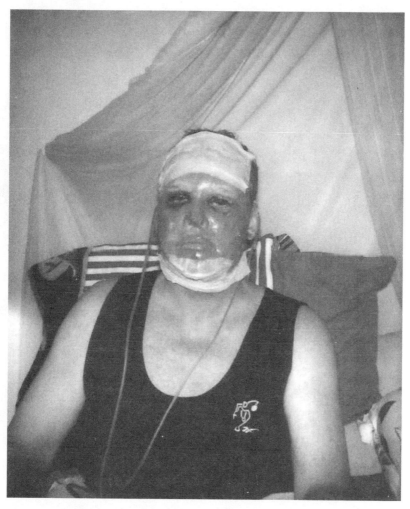

August 14, 1998—two days after the reconstructive surgery.

Fear and Loathing in Las Vegas, with Johnny Depp, Terry
Gilliam, and the crew. *(© 1998 Universal City Studios, Inc.
Courtesy of Universal Studios Licensing LLC)*

43. ODD

Other Dynamic Dimensions

JUST AFTER THE RECONSTRUCTIVE SURGERY ON MY FACE, I received an offer to do a cameo in the movie *Fear and Loathing in Las Vegas* adapted from Hunter S. Thompson's partly autobiographical novel based on his peculiar escapades. I got word that Johnny Depp would be playing Hunter S. Thompson and Terry Gilliam would be directing.

I'd casually met Johnny Depp a few times over the years, once while shopping for furniture at Shabby Chic on Montana Avenue in Santa Monica and a few times while visiting my agent (we were both with the same talent agency), but Johnny and I had never had the privilege of working together.

I knew Terry Gilliam not only for his hilarious work with Monty Python but also from a chance meeting at Warner Bros. four years earlier. I met Terry while visiting Mel Gibson and Dick Donner on the set of *Maverick*. At lunch with Terry, Mel, and a few other people in the Commissary Fine Dining Room, I started a food fight. I didn't mean to start a food fight; it just happened. Mel and I were in a festive mood as usual, carrying on to the extreme, joking with each other. He was eating pizza; I asked him for a slice, and he said, "Here, let me toss it to you."

I took his joke to the next level and shouted, "Food fight!"

Instantly, Mel and I stood up throwing food at each other. It didn't last long, but long enough to make an impression on Terry.

The script for *Fear and Loathing* was extremely odd in the best of ways. It captured Hunter S. Thompson to a T. I knew so because I had spent time with Hunter in Aspen. I met him outside a club owned by a friend of mine. We got along famously because Hunter was out there like I was—even more so. While speaking with Hunter, a feeling came to me that as a human being, Hunter received information from unearthly places that he utilized in his prose and speech. He rambled on about many things, all things bizarre. His ramblings from another dimension even had me stumped. As I listened to Hunter speak about life, I came to the conclusion that Hunter S. Thompson was a vivid experiment in humanity that will never be replaced or repeated again. He gave a new meaning to the word *eccentric*.

Being the oddball that I am, I felt privileged to be a part of this dynamically quirky team of players. I happily accepted the offer. I played the part of a highway patrolman who pulls over Raoul Duke, played by Johnny Depp, for speeding. We shot the scene at the top of a mesa that Terry found, where the rest of the crew could be down on the side, and out of sight. Terry, who was dressed like a sheikh, with a headband and long flowing white robe, explained the shot to me in great detail, then joined the rest of the crew at the bottom of the mesa and called, "Action!"

I did exactly as Terry explained. I pulled Raoul over, taking note of the odd items he had in his car (cases of beer, lightbulbs, stacks of towels, etc.). Then I asked him various questions as scripted and told him to go to a restaurant called Lucy's Hacienda to eat and take a nap. The scene was supposed to end there, but Terry didn't say, "Cut." I have a ritual; if I don't hear the word *cut*, I keep going. That makes the scene richer. It adds a dynamic dimension of improvisation. My improvisation can either be edited out or left in. So I stayed in character, lowered my voice, grabbed Johnny's face, and said, "Look me in the eyes." I stared at him for a long moment but said nothing.

Fear and Loathing in Las Vegas, with Johnny Depp. (© *1998 Universal City Studios, Inc. Courtesy of Universal Studios Licensing LLC*)

After a long beat, Johnny, still in character, asked, "Everything all right?"

I whispered, "May I have a kiss before you go? I'm very lonely here."

Now I can say, judging by my time spent with Hunter S. Thompson, that Johnny captured Hunter's essence to perfection. He gazed at me with those Depp eyes; something about his look gave me an odd impulse to pick him up and place him on the trunk of his car. Then I leaned in to kiss him. But before I got the chance—"*CUT! CUT!*" I heard Terry scream with lots of laughter. Terry quickly joined us on top of the mesa raving about our improv.

The next day, my agent called. "Just wanted to let you know Johnny Depp called to tell us what a great talent you are." That made me feel so good. After everything I'd been through, with cancer and then the reconstructive surgery, this movie was just what I needed.

Later, I heard that Hunter S. Thompson and the producers did not like the kiss improvisation, but Terry liked it, so it stayed in the final cut. Shoving Johnny on the car didn't make it, though. Then I heard, after Hunter watched the film a few times, that he changed his mind. He found it funny and right for the movie. The movie worked because Terry Gilliam's odd vision came from a 360-degree mirage straight from his heart. My advice: If Terry makes a movie, does a play, or even has an organ grinder's monkey collecting nickels on Sunday, *go see it.*

44. ART

Above **R**eal **T**ruth

I**N** 2004, I signed on to do an episode of a new HBO television show called *Entourage*. It was the sixth episode
of the first season, entitled, "Busey and the Beach." In the episode, the four main characters—Vincent, Drama, Eric, and
Turtle—attend my art show at an art gallery. Turtle accidentally knocks over one of my art pieces, destroying it. Then,
later at a Malibu beach party, Turtle apologizes to me for
breaking my sculpture. Simple enough.

When I got to the set, I asked the showrunner, Larry
Charles, "Where's the script?"

I could tell by Larry's joyful attitude that he loved what
he was doing. With a smirk, he said, "You are the script."

"What do you mean?"

"Make it up as you go." Larry, a freedom artist with
long, curly, dark hair, a beard, and a happy disposition,
who had previously worked on successful shows like *Sein-
feld* and *Mad About You,* had just given me free rein to do
what I loved most—improvise. Improv and spontaneity

have always been my forte. When you improvise, you have the freedom to be yourself and to allow the truth of your character to come from your heart. Usually, I wrap myself around the character, but now I didn't have to do that; I had total artistic freedom.

At *Entourage* third season premiere in Los Angeles, in 2007, with Adrian Grenier. *(Courtesy of Jeff Kravitz / Filmmagic.com)*

In the first scene, the set was a gallery filled with my paintings and sculptures made from circle art (white circles against a blue background). In the scene, I explain the inspiration of my artwork. I had no idea what the heck I was going to say. When the director, Julian Farino, said, "Action," I began rambling about how my artwork "evoked emotions from a discombobulated man" (I don't know where that came from). Then I continued jabbering about "emotional dyslexia, emotional confusion, and running na-

BUSEYISMS

ked through a cornfield backwards at midnight." I said all this ridiculous dialogue with a very honest, serious, straight face. When the scene was over, I heard a lot of laughter from the crew that I didn't expect, along with applause.

For the next scene, we shot at Topanga Beach. I asked Larry again, "Where's the script?"

I got the same answer, "You're the script."

I created a backstory for my character: He was an all-knowing ocean saint that could see through people's innocence. As luck would have it, I found a blue scarf lying on the beach, so I wrapped it around my head to signify my spiritual connection with the ocean. When the scene started, Turtle approached me on the beach and apologized for breaking my sculpture. I decided to educate Turtle about my ability to "loosen his teeth and snap his sternum with a quick head butt to the chest." Then I enlightened Turtle about art using quotes from my own life that I firmly believe to be true about art: "We are all here looking for the art within ourselves" and "Art is only the search; it is not the final form." I finished the scene by pouring a red bucket filled with water over Turtle's head, "cleansing him in the name of art and everything art stands for." I think the scene turned out good, although I don't think Turtle was too happy when I poured the water on his head.

Over the years, I did two more episodes, and they were more fun than ever. When the guys saw me on the set, I could hear them murmur, "Oh God, Busey's here; I wonder what he's going to do next."

Years later, I was trick-or-treating in Malibu West with my four-year-old son, Luke, when I ran into Kevin Dillon and his family. He told me they were working on the *Entourage* movie.

"I want to be in it," I said.

"Don't worry; we'll get you in it."

He kept his word. I got the call to do the movie and accepted. The day before I was set to shoot my cameo, I almost had to cancel because I was terribly sick with the flu, but because I had such fond memories of doing the television show, I forced myself to show up. When I saw Turtle on the movie set, he looked at me with disapproval. I have no idea if it was Turtle the character or Turtle the actor who was so cold, but that's okay; it's all in the name of art.

45. HOPE

Heavenly Offerings Prevail Eternally

O N MARCH 22, 2008, I was meeting my friend Terry in downtown Malibu at Bay Cities Beauty Store, where she was having her hair done. Terry, a former model I knew from Texas, needed a shoulder to cry on. She had just been through a brutal divorce from a rich dude that somehow left her sleeping in her car. When I entered the beauty supply store, I headed straight to the salon in the back to see Terry, but before I got there, a woman behind the counter caught my eye. She was a casually dressed woman in her thirties with a medium build, light brown hair, and a glowing smile. Although she worked in a makeup store that sold every beauty product under the sun, she wasn't wearing much of it. Her bright aura was like a beacon of light calling me closer, so I sauntered over to her.

The first thing I noticed was her business card on the counter that read *Steffanie Sampson, Certified Hypnotherapist* with a picture of her on it. I wanted to learn more, so I asked her about hypnotherapy. Her explanation was so pure and authentic. Her thoughts were grounded in metaphysics and spirituality. I had never met a woman like her before. She seemed so special. We only talked for ten minutes, but there was something that felt very familiar about her, so I took her business card.

Trying on hats at Disneyland with Steffanie Sampson.

At home, I set her hypnotherapy business card on my desk, constantly gazing at her picture smiling back at me. That picture! It shot right into my heart. She looked like an angel that hung around Peter Pan and Tinker Bell. But I just wasn't ready to speak to her on the phone yet. A few days later, I went back to Bay Cities Beauty Store to check on Steffanie. I found out that her family owned the store and she only worked on weekends. When Saturday rolled around, I found myself making excuses to go to the shopping center in Malibu where she worked. I told myself I needed to go to the eyeglass store, the shoe repair store, the bank, but really I was going down there to reconnect with Steffanie. When I saw her for the second time, she greeted me with that same bright smile. I bought a few cans of hairspray from her and asked more questions about hypnotherapy. It was another very nice, warm, and cordial meeting. Our encounter left me energized in a way I hadn't felt in years.

I found myself dropping in on Steffanie every weekend, buying some type of beauty product or asking different questions about hypnotherapy. All of a sudden, I realized, *Whoa, there's an attraction here.* I didn't really know what the attraction was except curiosity. Then I remembered a conversation I'd had the year before with my good friend and clairvoyant Michael Bodine. In our conversation, I had

With Michael Bodine. *(Courtesy of Michael Bodine)*

confided to Michael how very down I had become, how I felt I had betrayed myself in so many ways over my lifetime: crashing my motorcycle without a helmet, doing cocaine, marrying a stripper, being forced into my first marriage before I was ready. All my regrets had all piled up and were burying me alive. I continued to confide in Michael how lonely I was with no companionship and no hope of anything good on the horizon. Michael listened as he always did, then in his ever-cheerful way said, "Next year, in 2008, you are going to meet a soul mate."

"What's that going to be like?"

"When you look at yourself in the mirror, you'll see her reflection."

I didn't understand what Michael meant when he said that in 2007, but now I finally understood. He was talking about Steffanie.

I continued to visit Steffanie on the weekends at her store, and every time I did, I got a beautiful feeling of acceptance from her. I finally invited her to my house in Malibu. She thought she was coming to do hypnotherapy, but I just wanted to get to know her better. Instead, we talked for hours. It was the beginning of a great new friendship that grew quickly from then on. We either saw or spoke to each other on a daily basis. Everything was purely platonic.

On Memorial Day, I brought Steffanie to a beach party in Northern Malibu hosted by a real estate developer friend of mine. It was our first public outing together since we'd met two months earlier. We strolled the backyard of the lavish estate to a cliff overlooking the ocean, then took a path leading down to the beach. Halfway down the path, on a huge triangular rock off to the side, we discovered a king-sized mattress. It was a bizarre but welcoming sight. We got comfortable on the mattress and talked for a while. It was a very relaxed feeling of pure enjoyment with no agendas. Then I leaned over and gave Steffanie a kiss. I had never really tried to kiss Steffanie before. I mean, I gave her a peck here and there, usually when we said our hellos or good-byes, but those kisses were cold and flat on her part (like kissing the side of a car door). For some reason, on this special Memorial Day, the heavens opened up, and she kissed me back. It was a kiss that held so much meaning. It placed hope in my heart that we could move forward down a new path together.

With my daughter, Alectra Busey.

46. FAMILY

Feeling A Miracle In Loving You

S HORTLY AFTER I MET STEFFANIE, I moved from my
house on Coastline Drive in Malibu, where I lived for
almost twenty years, to a temporary apartment in Santa
Monica called the Sea Castle apartments. It was a much-
needed change of scenery. I was finally leaving the scene of
the crimes: the stripper, the drug overdose, the cancer—
everything that had been subconsciously bringing me down.
It felt as though I were crawling out of a deep dark hole, back
into the sunshine. My new apartment, which was located on
the third floor—room 307, to be exact—was tiny in size but
very mighty. Equivalent to a small hotel suite with a kitchen,
it was right on the beach in front of the Santa Monica Pier
with a sweeping view of the vast ocean. This part of Santa
Monica was bursting with lively energy, a nice contrast
from the quiet seclusion drowning me on Coastline Drive.
Every time I looked out the window, I got a different dose
of life swirling around me in all shapes and sizes. Exercisers
at Muscle Beach, families on the pier, bike riders, and

With Jake Busey.

Rollerbladers. It was a very fertile place and a very fertile time in my life with Steffanie.

Not only was Steffanie a hypnotherapist, she was also an aspiring actress with a nighttime waitressing job at the Chateau Marmont Hotel. The nights Steffanie wasn't waitressing at the Chateau Marmont, she was with me at the Sea Castle. I bought her a parking spot in my building; and I gave her some drawers in my one little dresser. She basically lived with me. Getting to know Steffanie on an intimate level was sheer joy. Steffanie was the significant replica of an angel that came to save me, resurrect me, and pull me back into a good life I thought I'd lost.

Steffanie used her hypnotherapy skills to point out the destructive patterns in my life that ultimately kept me from holding on to success. She believed they all stemmed from the abuse I encountered at the hands of my father, which she said left me with a subconscious feeling that I was unworthy of anything good. She also pointed out that every time I got to a place in my life of great success, I manifested something terrible to set me back, such as addictions, accidents, even illness to negate my success. The way Steffanie worked was very metaphysical. She was a self-proclaimed student of Louise Hay, constantly referring to Hay's book *You Can Heal Your Life* for reference. I couldn't quite grasp the concept of giving myself cancer until Steffanie pointed out some metaphysical facts: The sinus represented irritation toward one person; the left side of the body represented relationships; cancer represented deep hurt and resentment— all three of these pointed to my former second wife. I had to admit, it did add up. Steffanie had me thinking differently. She was also the only person who wasn't afraid to stand up to me or confront me on any bullshit I threw her way. In fact, she never let me get away with anything, which I respected immensely.

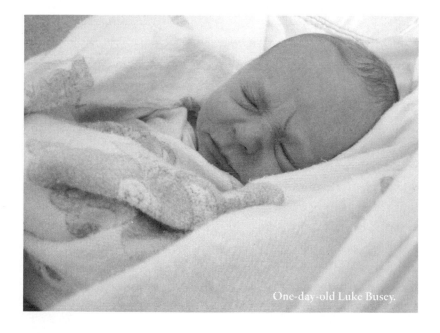

One-day-old Luke Busey.

Steffanie Sampson with Luke Busey. *(Courtesy of James Peragine)*

We loved to gaze at the pier. At this time, a new solar-powered Ferris wheel was under construction. It was fascinating to see the progress of its erection. When Steffanie was at work, I kept her apprised of its progress with "the Ferris Wheel Report," which was a three- to five-minute voice mail update done in a nasally character voice I named Smeck, designed to entertain Steffanie so she could slip away from work for a few minutes and have a good laugh. She boasted it was the highlight of her day.

Steffanie's favorite activity at the Sea Castle was Rollerblading. Every day, she was out there powering down the boardwalk for miles. When she returned, I always asked her a lot of questions so I could feel I'd been there with her. By April of 2009, Steffanie and I had been together for over a

With Luke Busey. *(Courtesy of James Peragine)*

year, and everything was still very light and happy, but when she returned from Rollerblading one day, she looked sad and distant.

"How was it today?" I asked.

"Awesome."

Her words didn't match her energy at all. "You seem sad. Did something happen?"

She didn't answer for a moment, then a tear dropped from her eye and rolled down her face. She said, "Gary, I've been thinking. I'm thirty-nine, and I want to have a child."

"You do?"

"Yes, I do. I want to have that experience. I want to have a baby."

"Okay, let's have a baby," I said automatically. Bringing a new soul into this world through our love felt natural to me (even though I was sixty-four years old).

"Okay!" Her demeanor changed on the spot as if a fifty-pound weight crushing her heart had been lifted.

At that point in my life, I had two children. Jake, from my first wife, Judy, and a daughter named Alectra from a relationship I'd had during my cocaine relapse. My addiction to drugs prevented me from being an ideal dad to both of them. I had many regrets. Now I was being given a third chance to be a good dad, and I took it. Steffanie got busy right away having acupuncture, drinking fertility herbs, and taking urine tests to find out when she was ovulating.

On May 31, 2009, Steffanie bounced into the room and with a very serious voice announced, "I'm ovulating! Come with me!" She grabbed my arm while stripping off her clothing and led me into the bedroom. On our way to the bedroom, Steffanie stopped at the window. "Let's invite a spirit in." We both held hands while looking up at the starry sky and said a prayer to our future child, inviting the spirit to join us on earth. Then we went to the bedroom and had the most incredible sex ever.

One month later while Steffanie was on her way to do hypnotherapy, she tracked me down at my favorite haunt, the Malibu Cigar Lounge. I was outside on the sidewalk when she pulled up waving a pregnancy test at me. "Look at this!" she raved. A plus sign on the stick boldly stared me in the face. "I'm pregnant!" she squealed. Then, as fast as she arrived, she was off to work, leaving me alone on the sidewalk. I wondered if I should tell the guys in the lounge or keep it to myself. I chose not to tell anyone. It was too sacred; I wanted to keep it close to my heart.

On our first and only attempt, we created Luke Samson Busey. Luke entered the earth's atmosphere at 6:40 A.M. on February 23, 2010, his exact due date. His first sound was a big *"Hey!"* announcing his arrival. Despite all the doomers and gloomers chastising me on the internet for having a child at sixty-five, I was blessed to create this new beautiful person. With this third chance at being a great father, by God, I was going to do it right. I was branded to be the best father in the history of the universe.

With John Rich and Dan Wheldon.
(Courtesy of Jeff Kravitz / Filmmagic.com)

47. FAILING

Finding An Important Lesson
Inviting Needed Growth

O N A LOVELY SUNDAY AFTERNOON IN 2010, I was invited to the Polo Lounge at the Beverly Hills Hotel for lunch with the producers of *The Celebrity Apprentice*. The show was already a guilty pleasure of mine since the season Joan Rivers made her appearance. After a colorful meeting with the producers, I discussed the pros and cons of doing the show with Steffanie. Ultimately, we decided it could be a great way to bring more awareness to traumatic brain injuries, so I agreed to do it. Earning money for charity was a very exciting prospect. Steffanie found the Center for Head Injury Services, a smaller charity in great need of donations. The center, located in St. Louis, Missouri, appealed to me greatly not only because they help people who have brain injuries but because they also help people who have autism, which I have always been passionate about. Leaving Steffanie alone with our six-month-old son for a month while I was on location in New York was tough. We'd recently moved from the Sea Castle apartments and were just settling into a cozy new home in Malibu, but I was up for the task.

In New York, I checked into the Trump International Hotel & Tower—room 1411, to be exact—and got ready to rumble. The schedule: Wake up at 5:00 A.M.; eat breakfast; hair and makeup; wardrobe with the fabulous Kitty Boots; find out our task; do the task; get home late; wake up early; complete the task; go to the boardroom; someone gets fired; repeat again from the beginning (hopefully).

In a nutshell, joining *The Celebrity Apprentice* was like going into a carnival blindfolded. You could hear laughter, people screaming, rides moving, balloons popping, guns blaring, and fireworks exploding (but you couldn't see them—just feel them). I spent the first two tasks getting myself in the groove of the show. They were mostly enjoyable for me, but enjoyable or not, that boardroom was cold as ice—like a frigidarium.

Each one of the judges had a distinct personality. Joan Rivers was funny, Ivanka was more insightful, Eric didn't say much, Donald Trump Jr. showed no emotion, and Donald Trump was Donald Trump. No warmth coming from him at all, although he did call me brilliant and a genius about twenty times. Their divisive questions seemed designed to fuel dissent aimed at creating chaos, and it worked. Chaos always ensued. Right off the bat, people got downright vicious in the boardroom.

By the third task, I felt confident I could win, so I volunteered to be project manager. In the challenge, each team had to create a camping experience display for Camping World. By now, my team was beginning to express animosity toward me. I constantly felt their resistance (except for

José Canseco), yet everything on the task went smoothly. I won. It was a glorious feeling to present Donna Gunning, head of the Center for Head Injury Services, a check for $20,000 along with $20,000 worth of camping gear. It was the highlight of my time on the show.

The patients at the Center for Head Injury Services.
(Courtesy of the Center for Head Injury Services)

Another highlight of this experience was a gift I received from the lovely and kind Marlee Matlin, who was on the opposing team. She noticed me struggling to hear all the time. After years of rock-and-roll music and the motorcycle accident (which caved in my hearing canal on the right side), I had been living with massive hearing loss for years but was unable to find a hearing aid that could stay in my ear properly.

"It's not right for you not to be able to hear; I want you to meet my friend at the Marriott Hotel in Times Square," Marlee said.

Marlee's friend, the incredible Dr. Bill Austin, leader of the Starkey Hearing Foundation (Marlee's charity), had the kindest and friendliest face I'd ever seen. His smile made me feel I was in the presence of someone as magical as Santa Claus; plus, he had thick white hair to boot. In his full booming voice, he said, "Gary, we're gonna fix your hearing today. When you leave here, you're going to be able to hear."

With Dr. Bill Austin at the Starkey Hearing Center for Excellence. *(Courtesy of Starkey Hearing Technologies)*

I didn't know what was going to happen, but if I could hear again, that would be a miracle. Bill tinkered around in my ears for a bit, then gave me tiny devices that opened up the world to me. As he'd promised, I was able to hear so well in that room in Times Square, I swore I could hear people unzipping their pants in California. It was like all my senses opened up automatically. My world changed from gray to Technicolor. I was alive in a whole new way, thanks to Marlee Matlin, Bill Austin, and the Starkey Hearing Foundation.

Aside from Marlee's kindness, there was no love coming my way from any of my teammates. By the fifth task, the team was blatant about not wanting me around, which hurt a lot. I didn't let the pain stop me. They were very irritated by many of my personality traits, but what the team most often complained about was my inability to focus. Anytime Mr. Trump asked them in the boardroom, "Who was your weakest player?" It was always, "Gary . . . Gary . . . Gary." They seemed determined to get me off the team.

For our fifth task, we created original artwork for sale. The team with the most money in sales would be the winner. After we shopped for art supplies, while settling into our workspaces, Meat Loaf, with the help of John Rich, scurried about looking for a bag of art supplies he'd lost. When he couldn't find them, Meat Loaf approached my workspace and asked me in a condescending tone if the paint I was using was really mine.

"Yeah, why?"

No reply.

Meat Loaf continued searching for his supplies, then, a brief moment later, he erupted like Mount Saint Meat Loaf, shrieking, *"FUCK! MOTHERFUCKER!"* His outburst seemed to come out of nowhere, which threw everyone for a loop. Then Meat Loaf continued shouting—at *me,* accusing me of stealing his art supplies. He shrilled various forms of profanity (mostly *motherfuckers*), then closed in toward me as if to fight while shooting a death stare my way. Mark McGrath restrained him. I calmly told Meat Loaf the supplies on my desk were the supplies I had bought. That flipped him out even more. The guys tried to placate him, but he was too enraged and past the point of no return. He screeched obscenities and threats while I stared at him unruffled, which sent him reeling. He threatened to put me in the hospital "in four minutes." Finally, Lil Jon joined Mark McGrath restraining him. As Meat Loaf continued his epic meltdown, John Rich ushered me out of the room, telling me not to engage. *Don't engage?* Come on, *of course* I'm not going to engage over *missing paint*—not a problem.

I went back inside to see what was going on just as John Rich happened to discover Meat Loaf's missing bag of art supplies on the floor in the corner of the room. Once Meat Loaf realized that I hadn't stolen his art supplies after all, instead of apologizing, he threw a can of spray paint at me and snapped (apparently he had helped himself to my supplies while I was out of the room), "Take your fucking spray paint."

"Thank you very much," I said coolly.

"Shut the fuck up! Do your fucking artwork and get outta my face!"

I was across the room. Honestly, I am not certain if this attack was a creation by my team on purpose to rattle me, or real, but during his monumental freak-out, I calmly stood still, like a military general with integrity and dignity, allowing Meat Loaf the freedom to snap and feeling very sorry for him.

Later that day, probably because the producers made him, Meat Loaf apologized to me, and I accepted. I understood things happened in this game that could upset you, but I also understood that if you allow yourself to get upset, you're going to fail yourself, like Meat Loaf did. I made it a point never to get upset with my teammates, even when they pushed me. We lost the art task, and surprisingly, Meat Loaf was not fired for his tirade. I can't imagine any company in the real world allowing that behavior, but with bad always comes good (if you're open to it); *Jimmy Kimmel Live!* created a hysterical Looney Tunes cartoon about Meat Loaf's meltdown, and I got to be Bugs Bunny (google it; it's funny).

Task after task, in the boardroom, the consensus continued to be that I had no focus and no skills. Mr. Trump asked the same question each time we were in the boardroom. "Who is the weakest member?" The answer continued to be, "Gary."

The word *failing* came to me a lot as my teammates persistently brought out my flaws. *All the disabilities I inherited from the motorcycle accident and secretly faced since my traumatic brain injury—my cognitive challenges with attention, concentration, processing information, understanding information, impulse control, distorted personal space, difficulty with balance.* The flaws that make me a good actor, but make others with brain injuries unemployable, left me feeling like a vulnerable loser in the school yard who was constantly being picked on by unevolved people with no greater understanding. But because of my spirituality, I didn't allow myself to take anything personally. Mr. Trump seemed to be the only one able to recognize any talents I had. When I finally got myself canned on the seventh task, Mr. Trump said, "Gary, you're very talented, you're very unique, you're an amazing guy, and, Gary, you're fired."

Being fired sent me into an internal panic. I failed. All my life, I have never given up or been able to accept defeat. The inside of my thighs and my forearms started cramping. When I got back to my hotel room, the cramping continued—all night. As I lay cramping in my room, I flashed on Donna Gunning with the Center for Head Injury Services. She had sent me a note that read, "Not only did your support provide critical dollars for survivors of brain injuries, but it also helped build morale among our staff, volunteers and the disability community here in Missouri." I realized I may not have won, but I hadn't failed. Yes, I got fired, but I made a positive impact on a lot of people in need. I understood that if you go for it, you can't fail. You might not get it right on the first try or the twentieth try, but eventually if you keep going, you find a better way to do it. There are always 360 ways to see an elephant. If you just put the elephant in the center of a circle and move around the circle one degree at a time, you'll see that same elephant in 360 different perspectives.

48. CHAMPION

Creating Happiness And Magical Progress In Overcoming Negativity

T HE BIRTH OF LUKE SAMSON BUSEY brought an immense bolt of energy, love, and happiness into my being, recharging my battery of life. For the first time, I was fully present, focused, and available, actively participating in my child's upbringing. Luke was the best little buddy I could ask for. He started walking at twelve months, exploring his surroundings with a fierce curiosity that reminded me of me. At fourteen months, he drove around in a baby scooter similar to the one I had as a child, with an uncanny ability to maneuver quickly around corners with the intensity of a stunt driver. Outdoors, he was always very happy. He loved to take long nature walks where he could discover bugs and pick flowers.

One particular windy Wednesday afternoon, on April 13, 2011, I was home watching yours truly promoting *The Celebrity Apprentice* on *The Ellen DeGeneres Show* while Steffanie and Luke were taking a walk. They had only been gone for about five minutes when they returned, which was very unusual. "Did you come back to watch Ellen with me?" I asked.

"No, Luke was acting funny; he didn't want to play."

I picked him up. He squirmed as if being touched made him uncomfortable. *Strange,* I thought. Steffanie took Luke into the kitchen. Moments later, she hollered, "He doesn't want to eat!" Also very strange. He was always a very big eater . . . just like his daddy.

"Maybe he's teething," I called back.

As the day progressed, it was pretty uneventful. Luke was not his usual robust self; he was lethargic, but not sick. When we put him to bed at his accostomed time, 7:00 P.M., he fell asleep quickly. Around 10:00 P.M., Luke started crying. He was such a happy baby he rarely *ever* cried, not even when he got hurt. I'd probably heard him cry only a handful of times. Steffanie picked him up to soothe him. "Oh my God!" she gasped.

"What?"

"He's on fire!"

In an instant, Steffanie's face went pale, and she started to panic. I had never seen Steffanie panic before. She looked like a lost little girl. In a flurry, she raced to the phone, carrying Luke in her arms, and called her mom. "Mom, Luke is burning up!" As Steffanie spoke to her mom, her voice quivered in agony. "And his heart is pounding through his chest! I can feel it!" Just then, white goo expelled abruptly from Luke's mouth. The vomit spewed uncontrollably, everywhere. It looked worse than *The Exorcist.* Steffanie wailed, "I don't know what to do!"

I ripped off Luke's pajamas. He was so hot it shocked me. I am not one to panic, but I knew in my heart something was terribly wrong. I told Steffanie, "Hang up with your mom and *call 911!* I don't want to lose him."

"Lose him?" Those two words shot through Steffanie like a bullet in the gut. She hung up immediately and called 911.

The paramedics arrived quickly, within three minutes, and began working on Luke. They informed us, "We need to take him to the hospital right now." Outside, red emergency lights flickered, cutting through the thick black Malibu sky. There were two large rescue trucks with an ambulance that Steffanie climbed into with Luke in tow. I followed behind the ambulance, like a driver from Stunts Unlimited, in our black Volvo family sedan.

We arrived at UCLA Medical Center, Santa Monica, within the hour, where they performed numerous tests on Luke to find out what was wrong. After six grueling hours of continual poking, prodding, and x-raying, they gave Luke a diagnosis of croup. He was treated with anti-inflammatory steroids, then we were sent on our way with a prescription to be filled. At home, we were so exhausted from the night, we crashed. Luke slept right between us in our bed. He seemed a lot better.

The next day, Luke woke up with a fever, but he was his usual hungry, energetic self. In the afternoon, Steffanie sent me to the pharmacy, then put Luke down for a nap. While I waited in a very long line at the local CVS pharmacy for the prescription, I got a call from Steffanie. The same agony from the night before was in her voice. "I called 911! Luke is . . ." She gulped.

"What?"

In bursts of emotion, she tried to get words out. "I don't know. He's crying . . . burning up . . . again. Wait a second.

They're here!" I heard a moment of commotion before Steffanie returned to the phone. "We're going back to the hospital. Forget the prescription; meet us there." I raced to my car and sped down Pacific Coast Highway until I caught up with their ambulance. We spent the rest of the day back in the emergency room at UCLA Santa Monica hospital until finally Luke had to be admitted.

We continued to be left in the dark—no answers, no diagnosis. Doctors continued administering tests, to no avail. By Friday, Luke developed a rash that covered his entire torso, conjunctivitis in his eyes, a strange-looking strawberry tongue with red spots, and red, dry, cracked lips, but worst of all, his high fever continued to persist. They filled his twenty-pound body with two types of antibiotics, trying to bring the fever down, but the fever wouldn't budge. It was like the fever was glued to Luke ever since that windy Wednesday night. When Saturday rolled around, without any explanation why our son was *burning up with fever for four days,* we decided to transfer him to Cedars-Sinai, where his pediatrician worked. As we were leaving UCLA, a doctor pulled us aside. "We think this is Kawasaki disease." We had never heard of Kawasaki disease before. Just the word *disease* put us off. There was no way that our fourteen-month-old son had a *disease* of any type. He had never had a sick day in his life.

As soon as we arrived at Cedars-Sinai, we met with Dr. Moshe Arditi, the director of Pediatric Infectious Diseases Allergy and Immunology. Dr. Arditi, a kind-looking man, took special interest in our case. His specialty was *Kawasaki disease.* There it was again, that damned Kawasaki disease. Dr. Arditi gave us a few basic facts about the disease: There is no laboratory test to diagnose it, the cause is unknown, it affects primarily boys up to five years of age, early symptoms can include fever that persists for five or more days, rash, conjunctivitis, strawberry tongue, red, dry, cracked lips, and irritability; *long-term effects are unknown.* There was no doubt in Dr. Arditi's mind; Luke had Kawasaki disease. He assured us that there was a simple treatment with a 95 percent success rate. Then, with a kind but firm bedside manner, Dr. Arditi gave us a very ominous statistic. "Time is of the essence! One in four children not treated within five to ten days of onset of fever can develop coronary artery aneurysms." *Aneurysms?*

Steffanie couldn't wrap her head around what was happening to our formerly healthy child. She reeled in a mind-boggling guessing-blame game as to why this was happening. "Maybe it's because I didn't breastfeed long enough. Maybe the thyroid medication I took when I was pregnant. Maybe the food I made him . . ." She spiraled into a tornado of doubt. But really none of that mattered. It was time to come to grips with the fact that our child had somehow contracted this mysterious, baffling *disease.*

On Sunday, April 17 (day 5), Luke was officially diagnosed with Kawasaki disease. Also on this day, the episode of my being fired aired on *The Celebrity Apprentice,* which meant I was contractually obligated to fly to New York to do press. Steffanie encouraged me to meet my obligation. She felt confident that everything was under control now that Luke finally had a diagnosis. She had her family, who lived ten minutes from the hospital, in the Hollywood Hills to lean on. I made her promise to keep me informed every step of the way while he received his treatment.

On Monday morning, April 18 (day 6), Luke had immunoglobulin therapy. The treatment of immunoglobulin seemed successful. Inside the unusually tall, prisonlike crib that housed our little champion, the IV drip of magic fluid coursed into Luke's body for eight hours or so, injecting him with new life. Almost immediately, he became his animated, happy little self again. After days of no appetite, he wanted to eat and drink milk. Best of all, after six days of fever, his temperature finally started to come down. But Steffanie was paranoid over one detail. She didn't like that the nurses took his temperature in the armpit. "They should do it rectally," she complained. Steffanie always rechecked Luke's temperature after the nurses did, using a rectal thermometer she brought from home, and every time, she got a higher reading by one degree. However, things were looking good. Over the next couple of days, Luke's temperature continued to slowly go down, then hovered at around 99.2, according to Steffanie's rectal thermometer. According to the hospital, his temperature was normal, so Luke was released on Thursday, April 21 (day 9).

Because of the rectal temperature of 99.2, Steffanie was not comfortable and did not feel Luke was out of the woods. "His temperature is normally 97.1, rectally, not 98.7, and certainly not 99.2. He still has a low-grade fever," she insisted. I gotta be honest here; I thought she was being overly paranoid. However, still suspicious this ordeal wasn't over, and since it was the weekend, Steffanie decided to stay with her family in the Hollywood Hills to be close to the hospital. As soon as she got there, Luke's fever began to rise. By morning, it was 99.5, sending Steffanie reeling into full panic mode *again*. On the phone, an on-call pediatrician tried to reassure her that a temperature of 99.5 was not anything to worry about, but Steffanie was adamant. "I know it's not much of a rise, but if he's better, it shouldn't

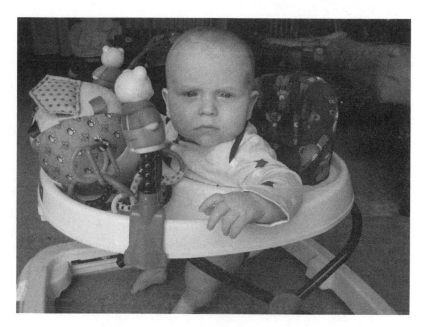

Luke Busey exploring the world in his baby scooter.

be rising at all. I know my child. I know there is something wrong." She took him back to the hospital and demanded a second treatment of immunoglobulin. Luke had received excellent treatment at Cedars-Sinai, but a mother knows best! On Saturday, April 23 (day 11), Luke had a second treatment. After four more days in the hospital, Luke's fever finally went down to *his* normal, 97.1.

Once the symptoms of Kawasaki disease are gone, you are still not out of the woods. Luke needed multiple echocardiograms over many years to be sure no aneurysms had developed, which was immensely stressful. Steffanie admittedly suffered from post-traumatic stress disorder after the ordeal. For years, every time Luke came down with a fever, Steffanie rushed him to the cardiologist, insisting they do an

Fun at lunch with Luke Busey.

echocardiogram to make sure no markers indicating Kawasaki disease were present. As of this writing, I am thrilled to report our champion Luke has been cleared by the cardiologist and never has to be checked for aneurysms again, and my champion Steffanie has recovered from her PTSD.

It was a very strange element of sickness for a little fourteen-month-old boy to face. When the challenge came (when my little guy got sick), my angels and spiritual guides let me know that he was going to be okay. I never doubted his recovery. I knew Luke had strong working angels helping him heal. In fact, after Luke's ordeal with Kawasaki disease, Steffanie and I frequently spotted flashes of glowing lights on his baby monitor flittering around Luke as he slept. We believe they were his angels protecting him.

Our ordeal with this bewildering disease inspired us to create the Busey Foundation for Children's Kawasaki Disease Research and Education. Kawasaki disease is the leading cause of acquired heart disease in children. When we started the foundation, we got endless emails telling stories of children who'd slipped under the radar, since most of the symptoms are synonymous with common childhood diseases, and consequently were not diagnosed in time to get proper treatment, thus developing coronary artery aneurysms. It is our hope that someday we can help to create a laboratory test so that no child goes undiagnosed within the essential treatment period of five to ten days and to gain a better understanding of the disease's long-term effects. To learn more, visit BuseyFoundation.org.

On the set of *Impractical Jokers* with Brian Quinn, Sal Vulcano, James "Murr" Murray, and Joe Gatto. *(Courtesy of Steffanie Sampson)*

49. LAUGH

Loving And Understanding
Goofy Humans

MY INNER CHILD'S LOVE for practical jokes started at an early age with the simple act of tickling. I loved how it made people contort their faces and jump out of their skin, but mostly I loved the way it made people laugh. As a child, my sister, Carol, claimed I couldn't pass her, my brother, or Mom in the house without tickling them. It's true. I always had to tickle somebody. Carol maintains I loved the sound of tortured laughter. The truth is I enjoyed it because instinctively I knew laughter was good for them.

In my formative years, at my Christian youth group, there were always parties. At these parties, watermelon was usually served. The great thing about watermelon, besides its delicious flavor, is the juicy seeds. I loved to see how many seeds I could stick in someone's hair, face, or clothing. With my surefire technique, I put the seed between my thumb and index finger and squeezed as hard as I could, sending it shooting in the air like a mini rocket directly at my target, usually the forehead. The stickiness of the watermelon juice assured the seed would cling wherever it landed. One time, I don't know how, I shot a seed inside the nostril of a girl named Evelyn Keyes. It went so far up her nostril she couldn't get it out. People surrounded her with tweezers and different types of paraphernalia trying to help her. Ultimately, it came out with the tweezers.

Over the years, it was my inner child that made me seem funny, smart, and philosophical. It won me the award for best personality in junior college. At college, it was very easy for us athletes to get bored. One day, we decided to eat as many beans as we could and fart into mason fruit jars stuffed with wax paper. We stored the fart jars in our dorm room for about three weeks. When we felt they were ready, we took the fart jars to the student union (which was heavily populated with people talking, studying, playing cards, etc). We set the jars down, uncapped them, pulled out the wax paper, then sprinted to a hidden location where we could watch the action unfold as the stench of our farts circulated into the noses of the unsuspecting college students. Even from afar, we could smell the foul odor. To our surprise, the smell was so heinous, people ran for cover. It cleared the student union in eight seconds. This was by far our most potent prank of all.

Because of our diets, the football players had a lot of flatulence. I'm not quite sure whose idea it was to light our farts on fire, but I would probably guess it was mine. The farter lay on the bed, pants down, legs in the air, with his butt hanging over the edge of the bed. The fartee placed a lighter below the awaiting bum. As soon as the farter felt his gas ready to blow, he'd shout, "Here it comes!" If the timing was perfect, we lit the fart just as it left the rump, causing the flame to shoot out, then get sucked directly back inside the anus of the farter. The reaction: howling laughter and panic (sometimes the underwear caught fire, too).

Don't even think about trying this in the privacy of your own home.

Farting is very funny—the sound, the smell, sometimes the taste. Farting is a Universal Truth. No matter what language you speak or don't speak, you understand what is being said with a fart. It allows the freedom of gut-wrenching laughter with someone you normally might not have shared a laugh with. I've noticed this primarily in elevators.

When I came across the show *Impractical Jokers* on truTV sometime in 2014, I laughed so hard I couldn't breathe. If you haven't seen it before, it is a hidden-camera show where four lifelong friends, Brian "Q" Quinn, James "Murr" Murray, Joe Gatto, and Sal Vulcano dare each other to do asinine things to strangers with the hopes of embarrassing each other. If they don't take the dare, they lose. Their goofy, buffoon-like antics are what initially socked me in the gut. They reminded me of *me*. *Impractical Jokers* quickly became a favorite show for my entire family—even four-year-old Luke. Eventually, I met the Jokers on Twitter, which led to a friendship.

In 2016, I signed on to do a part in the longest-running play in New York history, *Perfect Crime*. I let Murr know I was in his hometown, the Big Apple. To my delight, he invited me to make a secret cameo on *Impractical Jokers,* unbeknownst to everyone else on the show. My schedule was very tight, but the joker in me could not refuse a good laugh.

Only two people knew I was coming—Murr and a producer. I arrived on the set in the middle of Manhattan, two hours before my *Perfect Crime* curtain call, with no idea of what I was going to do. Murr said, "Trust me, this is gonna embarrass the hell out of Sal and shock the whole crew." He quickly explained the prank: While Sal is conducting an interview, unbeknownst to the interviewee, surprise Sal through a two-way mirror and make him laugh. Murr was dressed in a white lab coat à la Bruce Banner from *The Incredible Hulk*. I was dressed in a ripped white lab coat with insane hair à la the Hulk from *The Incredible Hulk*. Murr drank a vial of green fluid, then gagged. The two-way mirror went dark. I quickly switched places with Murr. When the two-way mirror went clear again, I shocked the hell out of Sal, the Jokers, and the crew as Murr had promised. It was glorious to see everyone lose it. I do the show whenever I get the opportunity. Now I consider myself the fifth Joker on standby.

50. END

Exciting New Direction

E VER SINCE I SAW WALT DISNEY'S *Peter Pan* in 1953, I knew, in my nine-year-old mind, that I was Peter. Just like Peter, I have always been a free spirit with a mischievous streak. My wild nature, along with a sense of immortality, has carried me to magical places that, at times, have taken me far away from safety. For some reason, I have never had a desire to be safe. I have gone up, down, and sideways, and I wouldn't change a thing, not even the motorcycle accident. That is shocking for people to digest. Some claim the motorcycle accident damaged my brain or made me insane. I can understand why some might feel that way.

It is my feeling that the accident gave me an opportunity to be in the most loving place possible, the supernatural. It altered my brain in a way that gave me a different perspective on life. In this heavenly place known as "the other side," I felt feelings of unconditional love so powerful, there are no words to describe it. Those feelings are still in my heart and have colored my life like a rainbow ever since.

I am not breaking the bank like I did in my younger days,

but that's okay. Material possessions aren't as important to me as they once were. The most important thing (besides good health, of course) is giving and feeling love. That is priceless.

Now in my seventies, I live in a multidimensional world filled with unpredictable wonders. I have no fear of death; I know life goes on. There is no end. The end is only the beginning. However, since this book has to stop somewhere, I would like to take this opportunity to thank you for reading the stories of my life. I hope they have been motivational and inspirational for you. Let me leave you with a suggestion: Go slow and let nature take you, and everything you see will be a reflection of yourself.

With Love Signing On,
Gary

I go to my window, look into the darkness, and
see light reflect down deep in my eyes. Like a
snowflake from heaven, love sits on my shoulder.
I won't see it, but it is with me all night.
"Freedom" is the key to forever. You may not
know it, but you hold the key *now* because it
was placed in your soul when you were born.

—*Gary Busey*

Epilogue. FOUND

Focused On Understanding
Natural Direction

NOVEMBER 10, 2010
"FOUND on Bonsall"

A grand house in the woods near the ocean,
a rider is coming to see.

Through the fog, the mist, and the shadows of night.

With sounds of the dark he can taste and feel.

Tooting, growling, scraping, and sawing
on the path to the house in the woods.

His steed is protected, his sword it is sheathed,
and his eyes on all that is around.

Time matters not when the arrival comes to the
connection of connections ever more. And that,
my friend, is to be FOUND.

—Gary Busey

I would rather have the memory of a lost
kiss than no memory of a kiss forgotten.

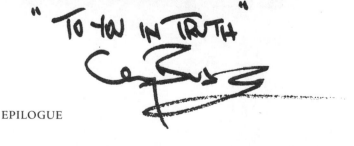

"TO YOU IN TRUTH"

Throwing the first pitch for the Tampa Bay Rays.

Acknowledgments

I would like to thank all the people who have helped shape my life:

To my amazing children, Jake, Alectra, and Luke, thank you for understanding and loving me just as I am.

To my father, D.L. Busey, my mother, Virginia S. Arnett Busey, my sister, Carol, my brother, David, and the entire Busey, Booth, and Stuart families, thank you for helping me become the man I am today.

To my partner, Steffanie, thank you for urging me to write this book, and motivating me to go deeper into the experiences of my life.

To my wonderful editor, Marc Resnick, a special thanks for your uplifting support during this process, it means the world to me.

To my mentor, Mr. James Best, who taught me film awareness and camera technique, thank you for everything.

To Michael Bodine who always helps guide me in a beautiful, spiritual, brotherly way, thank you forever.

To my first wife, Judy Lynn Helkenberg, who, in every way, helped me get my career started, thank you.

To my Nathan Hale line coach, Larry Miller, thank you for helping me find my courage so I could play like a champion.

To my Nathan Hale head coach, H. J. Green, thank you for teaching me how to use my energy and drive to be the best starting center I could be.

To my O.S.U. theater arts teacher, Vivica Locke, thank you for teaching me the essence of theater and the truth of my heart.

To Karin Gutman Orloski, thank you for your help in the creation of this book.

To the "Busey Team" that keeps me going every day, I am eternally grateful.

Finally, I would like to thank all my earthly relations who have helped me along the way. From deep in my heart to everyone I have met, thank you all for your love and patience. Please know I love you back.

Glossary of Buseyisms

ACTION—**A** Confident Transition In Overcoming Negativity

ACTOR—**A** Channel That Offers Research

AGE—Λ Growing Evolution

ALIEN—**A** Living Intuitive Energy Nearby

ALIVE—**A**lways Living In Victorious Energy

ANGEL—**A** Nice Guiding Energy Loves

ANGER—**A**nother Negative Grievance Explaining Rage

APE—**A** Precocious Energy

ART—**A**bove Real Truth

ARTIST—**A** Real Tower In Seeking Truth

AWESOME—**A** Wonderful Experience Showing Others Magnificent Energy

BABY—Being A Beautiful You

BAD—Bologna And Dirt

BADASS—Bologna And Dirt And Something Sweet

BAND—Bringing A New Direction

BANKRUPTCY—Bringing A New Knowledge Regarding Understanding Past Tribulations Concerning Yourself

BEAUTY—Be Exciting And Understanding To Yourself

BELIEVE—Bring Essential Love In Every Victory Experienced

BIRTHDAY—Being Invited Righteously Through Heaven Divinely Announcing You

BLAME—Being Loud And Making Excuses

BOXER—Bringing On X-Rays Every Round

BULL—Bringing Up Life Lessons

BULLY—Bad Ugly Loud Lost You

CALM—Carrying A Loving Mind-set

CAN—Creative And New

CAN'T—Creating A Negative Thought

CARE—Creating A Right Effect

CAT—Conniving And Tactical

CEO—Chief Enabling Officer

CHAMPION—Creating Happiness And Magical Progress In Overcoming Negativity

CHANGE—Creating Happiness And New Guiding Energy

CHAOS—Critical Hate And Overwhelming Stupidity

CHILD—Candid Honesty In Loving Doses

CLARITY—Celebrate Life And Rituals In Trusting Yourself

CLOWN—Creating Laughter On Wednesday Nights

COURAGE—Constantly Outpouring Uplifting Radiant Awesome Giving Energy

COW—Come On Woman

COWARD—Counting On Weak And Ridiculous Decisions

CREATE—Cultivating Right Energy And Terrific Effects

DAD—Dedicated And Devoted *or* Dumb And Dumber *(Depends on the Dad)*

DANCE—Discovering A Natural Creative Expression

DARE—Doing A Radical Experiment

DAY—Dream Another You

DEATH—Don't Expect A Tragedy Here

DEBT—Don't Expect Big Things

DENIAL—Don't Expect New Information About Life

DESTINY—**D**irected **E**nergy **S**upporting **T**ravel **I**n **N**ew **Y**ears

DIVINE—**D**ealing **I**n **V**ictory **I**n **N**atural **E**xploration

DIVORCE—**D**uo **I**n **V**iolation **O**f **R**omantic **C**reative **E**nergy

DOG—**D**umps **O**n **G**round

DOUBT—**D**ebating **O**n **U**nderstanding **B**ewildering **T**houghts

DR.—**D**oing **R**ight

DRAG—**D**on't **R**efuse **A** **G**irl

DREAM—**D**etails **R**evealing **E**xcitement **A**nd **M**agic

DRUNK—**D**rinking **R**ecklessly **U**nderstanding **N**othing **K**ind

EARTH—**E**xploring **A** **R**itual **T**ribal **H**appening

EASTER—**E**arth **A**ngel's **S**tory **T**o **E**mpower **R**esurrection

EASY—**E**xperience **A** **S**imple **Y**ou

END—**E**xciting **N**ew **D**irection

FAILING—**F**inding **A**n **I**mportant **L**esson **I**nviting **N**eeded **G**rowth

FAITH—**F**antastic **A**dventures **I**n **T**rusting *Him*

FAMILY—**F**eeling **A** **M**iracle **I**n **L**oving **Y**ou

FART—**F**eeling **A** **R**ectal **T**ransmission

FEAR—**F**eeling **E**xposed **A**nd **R**ejected

GLOSSARY OF BUSEYISMS

FEELINGS—Finding Elevated Emotions Living Inside Now Generating Sensations

FILM—Feelings Illuminated Like Magic

FIRED—Forced Into Reality/Retirement Excuses Denied

FISH—Floating In Sea Houses

FLOAT—Feeling Light On Air Today

FLOW—Finding Loving Order Within

FLY—First Love Yourself

FORGIVE—Finding Ourselves Really Giving Individuals Valuable Energy

FORWARD—Finding Ourselves Really Willing And Really Driven

FRAUD—Finding Relevant Answers Under Deception

FREEDOM—Facing Real Exciting Energy Developing Outta Miracles

FUN—Finally Understanding Nothing

FUTURE—Finally Understanding Totally Unlimited Resources Everywhere

GIFT—Guidance In Future Travel

GOAL—Go On And Live

GOD—Good Orderly Direction

GUIDE—Giving Understanding In Detailed Experience

GUILT—Giving Up Inspired Loving Thoughts

GUITAR—Gaining Understanding In Tunes And Rhythm

GURU—Giving Us Real Understanding

HABIT—Holding A Bewildering Interest Today

HAPPY—Holding A Positive Perspective Yearly

HAT—Hiding A Toupee

HATE—Holding A Treacherous Energy

HEAL—Holding Energy And Light

HEALTHY—Holding Energy And Light To Help Yourself

HEART—Honor Expression And Real Truth

HOME—Holding Our Memories Eternal

HONEST—Having Open Nature Explaining Sincere Truth

HOPE—Heavenly Offerings Prevail Eternally

IT—Indian Time

JOY—Jolly Optimistic You

KIND—Keeping It Nice Daily

LAUGH—Loving And Understanding Goofy Humans

LAW—Losers And Winners

LIE—Living In Excess

LIFE—Living In Forever Eternity

LIGHT—Living In God's Heavenly Thoughts

LIVE—Learning In Volcanic Energy

LOVE—Living On Victorious Energy

MAD—Making Another Detour

MAGIC—Miracles And Gifts In Creation

ME—Most Excellent

MEAN—Making Everything Absolutely Nasty

MIND—Making It New Daily

MIRACLE—Moving Into Rapturous Angelic Cosmic Loving Energy

MOM—Made Of Magic

MONKEY—Manic Offbeat Nature Keeps Entertaining You

MOTIVATION—Moving Our Thoughts Into Victory And Truth In Overcoming Negativity

MUSIC—Magnificent Unique Sound Inviting Creativity

NAG—Now A Grinch

NAP—Not A Possibility

NASCAR—Non-Athletic Sport Centered Around Rednecks

NEAT—Nice Exciting And Tight

NEWS—North East West South

NO—Never On

NOW—No Other Way

NUTS—Never Underestimate The Spirit

ODD—Other Dynamic Dimensions

OLD—Our Love Deepens

PANIC—Planning Another Negative Issue Constantly

PAST—Preoccupation About Spent Time

PATIENCE—Projecting Accepting Thoughts In Every New Challenging Experience

PEACE—Purely Experiencing A Comfortable Energy

PIG—Plays In Garbage

PLANET—Projecting Life And New Entities Throughout

PLAY—Please Laugh At Yourself

POOP—Pushing Out Old Produce

PRAY—Planning Right Answers Yourself

RELAPSE—Really Exciting Love Affair Perfecting Self-Extermination

RELATIONSHIP—Really Exciting Love Affair Turns Into Overwhelming Nightmare Sobriety Hangs In Peril

ROMANCE—Relying On Magnificent And Necessary Compatible Energy

RUDE—Really Upsetting Demeanor Expressed

SAD—Seeking Another Defeat

SELF—Seeing Everything Loving Forever

SELFISH—Showing Extremely Lavish Feelings In Self-Hoarding

SHAME—Seeing How A Mistake Expands

SIMPLE—See It Manifesting Precious Loving Energy

SIN—Self-Imposed Nonsense

SMILE—Showing Magnificent Inner Loving Energy

SOBER—Son Of a Bitch Everything's Real

SORRY—Sending Out Retractions Regarding Yourself

SOUL—Showing Others Unconditional Love

SPIRIT—Seeking Proper Instructions Regarding Intimate Truth

SPORT—Seeing People On Respectable Teams

STOP—Stand To On Purpose

STRIPPER—Standing Tall Revealing Intimate Private Parts Expecting Remuneration

STRONG—Stretching To Reach Opportunities Not Given

SURF—Standing Up Riding Free

TRANSFORMATION—To Reach And Not Stop For Open Rescues Made And Taken In Offerings New

TRUST—Talking Realistically Understanding Sacred Truth

TRUTH—Taking Real Understanding To Heart

TRY—Tomorrow's Really Yesterday

VIP—Very Important Primate

WAR—Women And Religion

WIFE—Wanted In Forever Eternity

WIN—Wanting It Now

WORRY—Working On Ridiculous Routines Yearly

WOW—Walking On Water

WRONG—Working Righteously On Nothing Good